NEW PONY:

A HORSE LESS ANTHOLOGY

# NEW PONY:
# A HORSE LESS ANTHOLOGY

Edited by Jen Tynes and Erika Howsare

# TABLE OF CONTENTS

"It will not be said that the hippopotamus and elephant came always to the same spot, the former to deposit his grinders, and the latter his tusks and skeleton. For what became of the parts not deposited there?"

- Thomas Jefferson, from *Notes on the State of Virginia*


"They say you're usin' voodoo, your feet walk by themselves
They say you're usin' voodoo, I seen your feet walk by themselves..."

-Bob Dylan, "New Pony"

# Insect Wildlife

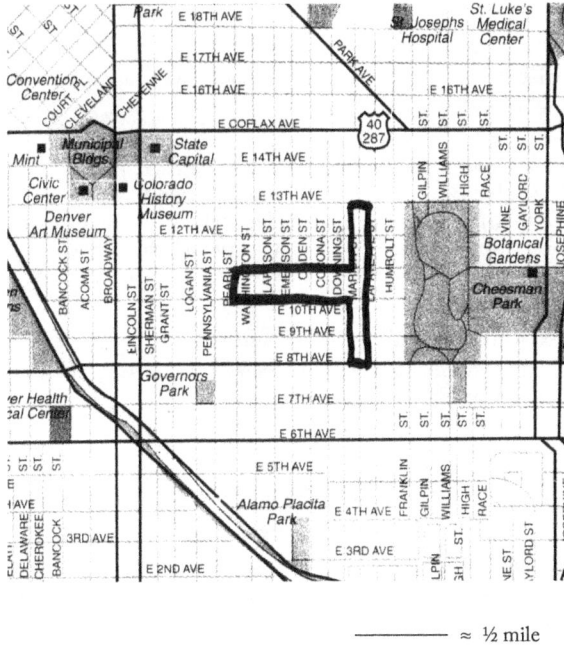

——————— ≈ ½ mile

*There is a spell, for instance,*
*in every sea-shell*

H.D.

"That's like stenciling," Susan tells me. So I make my "T" into a giant stencil "T," one that, if I were to make the top of the map the top of the page, would be lying on its stomach. She walks with me this time, and we notice lots of things in alleys like the remnants of a fire: burnt Simon and Garfunkel records, a charred rocking chair, probably antique, with a blackened TV on it, a wet book with browned edges (either self-help or pulp), and a planner opened to July 8th that reads "Nicole's Birthday."

We see black marks (another fire?) like gouache on an old carriage house, Baudelaire's face in green spray paint on a fence, and a funny design like a snake doubling back on itself, again and again, which she correctly identifies as glue for a long gone sign. "No Parking," we wonder, or maybe, "Beware of Dogs." There are a lot of dogs in this alley, we think, and a lot of dog shit in the little canyons made by melting ice.

*

In our house, there's an etching done by a third-grader. He hasn't signed the piece, but his name has been written in on the back along with an explanatory note not unlike a Certificate of Authenticity. It reads:

> This artwork has been created and donated by the artist: Jakob. Students learned the art form of printmaking. Artists experienced the technique of ETCHING. The process included etching onto a foam plate then inking and printing the image. Please enjoy this wonderful gift of creativity. Your purchase will help support the visual arts program at *X Elementary*.

He's called it "Insect Wildlife," only I can't find any insects in it. And although there is a snail in the bottom right corner, a snail's not an insect, it's a gastropod—a mollusk with a coiled shell.

The etching has tracings of Jakob's hands, which are supposed to look either like trees or rocks. I've been thinking lately about how bodies try to make things that look like trees or rocks and how the rocks or trees still look like bodies made them. How a body is implicated in the making of things like trees or rocks, how it plays its game of hide-and-seek within the made. But, in an age of quiet things and quiet makers, can a body be too cautious?

I've also become obsessed with strips of concrete: the signatures contractors leave on the sidewalks—*Laid by Larry, 1954*, etc. I am always surprised to remember I am walking on someone else's life. As though a snail had died and left behind, like a little monument, this abandoned shell, this curious secretion of chitin, hardened with calcium carbonate.

*

A poet in town for a reading last week told me over a bowl of black bean soup that in Salt Lake City it is possible to live on 13000th Street. I look it up. It's true. Although technically you're in the south suburbs at that point. The streets, she told me, are numbered according to how far away from the Mormon Tabernacle you are. It's a helpful mnemonic: say you're trying to give directions to the Tabernacle from 8001st St. *It's 8000 blocks that way*, you can say.

The Mormon Tabernacle's shaped like an egg inside—Brigham Young is said to have gotten the design by staring at an eggshell—and is so acoustically sensitive that you can hear a pin dropped in the pulpit from the back of the hall. Its structure mimics the city's (or is it the reverse?): you can orient yourself to the Tabernacle as to the pin in the pulpit.

Put another way, the Tabernacle is the city's signature, the stamp impressed into each of the city's corners, the predominant sign by which it is known. As with the name stamped into the sidewalk, the city's streets indicate their origin at each turn, the Ur-place signified on the other side of every sign.

*

A good signature, or so my elementary school art teacher told me, is part of being a good artist. And it's true that some painters are good signers of paintings. Paul Klee, at least on first glance, wasn't one of them: his signatures are inconsistently placed and sometimes don't show up at all.

"Blossoming" (1934) is a late variation on Klee's grids, painted when he returned home after having been forced from his post at a German art school the year before. Its grid is less rigorous than in earlier paintings: its lines wavier and its blocks, in terms of their variation in size and shape, like the aesthetically pleasing stone slabs you see sometimes, when walking down sidewalks, in place of concrete.

The outer blocks of the painting are larger, earthier in color. Browns, dark reds, tans and maroons predominate, but as you move closer to the center the blocks get smaller and brighter: yellows, oranges, light blues and greens burst out at you. Some blocks are all white and you think: petals.

Klee's tag appears at the very top of the painting, not in the center block, which is the fifth one in, moving from either the right or left edge, but just off-center. It's tentative. An afterthought. Its hold on the proceedings is minimal, tangential. As if Klee didn't want us to know he'd been there and even though we can still see him: his hands left their traces in the lines.

It's true that contractors don't always sign their sidewalks either, or they're inconsistent: there never seems to be a reason why they've stamped one square and not another. The practice on a whole seems to have died out somewhat—most days I only find dates up to the early 80s—unless there's been a moratorium on new sidewalks.

It's possible the names are still there, embedded in each square of concrete. That, like the Tabernacle haunting far corners of Salt Lake City, one walks on the names of dead men and women, buried in the aggregated gravel, limestone, water, and sand. Possible, too, that such lives are embedded in everything hewn by human hands. That, like the recombinant strands of genes present in each of our body's variegated cells, the dead comprise a different sort of genetic material, and that they speak to each other in dulcet tones through the steel bars supporting our bridges, the fabric lining our couches, the spines supporting our books.

But it's more likely that the names disappeared with the bodies they belonged to when those bodies became the things they made, or rather, the things they made became them. This is fine if a body makes music, but if it makes a wall, that's tougher. A body can move to music, but it can't move to a wall, unless it has stopped moving.

*

In Paul Auster's book, *City of Glass*, a character named Peter Stillman, convinced "The story of the Garden [of Eden]…records not only the fall of man, but the fall of language," traces the words "TOWER OF BABEL" on his afternoon walks in Manhattan. He gives names to the broken, dented, and crumpled objects he finds. He wants to imbue the degraded world with new meaning, he says, and so retreats to a time when the world was new and Adam was naming. He argues that it's "our duty as human beings to put the egg back together again"—the linguistic egg that has, like Humpty-Dumpty, fallen from its wall.

But a pristine egg isn't really an egg: the linguistic egg cannot be put back together again because an egg is made to be broken. Stillman never sees that words are inherently a retreat, and, thus, "to be a poet," as Raymond Williams writes, "is, ironically, to be a pastoral poet"—one who retreats from the world to its symbols, as though all of language were the field in which, like shepherds singing to their beloveds, the objects of our expression are to be praised but never touched. Words only take their place in the house of Being Heidegger thought language was when they cease to imitate objects, when they acknowledge their distance, as though measured in thousands of blocks, from the objects they intend. And yet, our words contain the traces of any number of things: in them we might hear, however faintly, pin drops in pulpits.

*

The detection of an object can, paradoxically, result in a kind of effacement. Before disappearing completely, the "detective" assigned to trail the elder Stillman (a writer of detective novels named Quinn), sequesters himself in a lonely alley for a seemingly interminable stakeout. He emerges transformed—so much so that he no longer recognizes his reflection in the mirror.

Likewise, one writes oneself into being at the expense of the self. The text comes to know its writer—it records him—even as it erases the person he has been. So this text keeps company with an unrecognizable version of myself, which is to say: I cannot recognize myself in the text. Like Quinn, who records the events of City of Glass in a red notebook, I may disappear when the text is complete—when there is no longer any room to write.

But if I do not want to disappear?

*

Francis Ponge's poem, "Notes Toward a Shellfish," begins with a retreat into "the form of the shell," which Ponge says he prefers to "the temple at Angkor, Saint-Maclou, or the Pyramids." The shell, he writes, is "more mysterious than these all too incontestable human products." But there's a strange turnabout in the poem: after wishing that people would produce such shells—products more suited to the size of their bodies—Ponge writes that he admires "above all the writers, because their monument is made of the human mollusk's true secretion, the thing best proportioned and adapted to his body, though inconceivably dissimilar in form: I mean LANGUAGE." Writing or speaking, Ponge implies, we're in our most "natural" state: language is always already pastoral. For language, we ought to read country. Or, as Elizabeth Willis has written, "for word, read world."

An abandoned shell is an empty, calcareous husk. But shells, like ruins, also overwhelm with the lives of those who inhabited them. Life's animation secretes a thin glaze that gathers over the inanimate object, an aura emanates from within.

Language is such a shell. Distrust it though we may, once lived in—once cared for, cultivated, and loved—it will always bear the marks of our existence. No matter how far we run to hide from our names—our own or of things—our responsibility follows us. Spectral presences stalk us in words as in works. Because there is a kind of spell in a seashell, a stamp left on the made, and we operate under that spell. It is to those presences that our debts—which are our distances—must be paid.

*

When I moved to Denver, I started noticing a lot of ghosts in sheets with jagged hems in the neighborhood. A ghost, I thought. How appropriate. The faces were different, but the tag was the same. Consistently placed and consistently drawn, it was the most practiced, most studied, part of the routine. Then again, much graffiti is only a tag—the division between maker and made breaks down, and as a result there's little difference: a sidewalk, a name. A wall. Having stopped moving.

A poem, Williams famously stated, is a machine made out of words. But though its character may be physical, art becomes mechanical at a cost which is nothing less than its evacuation. For, if art is a machine, it is one we wear on our person, like a skin:

through it, we respire. Without our animation, it is nothing. Not even a relic, not even a ruin.

Though we figure in what we make, the making can get lost in the made, since nothing can become a name without stopping. Without distancing itself from its source. But no less than a word, a name is a pin drop. Try though we might to ignore it, it's almost as though the poem had a pulse.

So to write is to walk all over the word. And you can see how you could do this—how you could walk all over your name.

## Cynthia Arrieu-King & Kristi Maxwell

## First Field

Deer stooped like grass in prayer.
Clobbered with asking, ears that field the pleasing side
of a head.

Given a slippery hoof, given a large
philosophy to spread into loss,
there was speculation, "Fire?" An underside
to each sigh, an underbrush

& moon necking with sea grass
deer as swoon the field boasts
bonfire,
sure—

Why have we? Or: where are the laws?
The animals are strapped to the look. Are pauses there.
Such informers
uniformed tan by a maker

to slink between a graze and a shrug.

\*

Noon led the sun, muzzle-like, down.
Whole nostrils of light.
We stuff. Call me taxidermist again;
please tack deer to mist and quiz me.

Pantries of so-so are sopped up
by an eye for an eye
lidded by a pan.

Vibration that trims each bell.
A shell shrugs its velveteen

station that we call each ear –
some voice does chug there.
Hammock and muck. A hoof: the last today

to mark a beach.
Scent swings the mock-up forest up and forth.

*

A car drives on across the evening, cursor between here and there. Bling of light.
Night lies over everything, the bonfires small as mosquitoes, so far.
Legions of temporary deer, the antlers of towers, static.
They have been doing exactly as they should be doing.

And we?

Should slow the plan.
An overnight rate
Is a window unwanted.
To ban, to clean. A weapon.

Deer is a city. Deer is a distance. Deer acidic and splotch.
Deer seedy-eyed and ample and thus we go in.
Deer is debate, so have it:

A silence
That fits like meat.
De lime, de lime.
That delineates.
That.

**Sarah Bartlett & Emily Kendal Frey**

## After Keats

Women's stubbled legs, whorled patterns on skirts,
men in khaki or olive or other states of green:

we're wearing spring. But when I look at faces
it's disappointing. They're just faces. Sexy and ugly

work categorically. Tomorrow I'll paste blossoms
over my eyes and carry cups of water to splash them with.

I'll be the season even if I have to fake it.
The man selling tulips at Back Bay has a new sign:

Flowers Survive Existential Crisis. Any one of us could
suddenly open, display delicate pistils, and shoot.

**Sarah Bartlett & Emily Kendal Frey**

# EVENT HORIZON (1)

The woman next door is an astronomer.
She leaves each morning dressed
in pinstripes, hair neatly
twisted at the nape. I watch for her
entrances and exits but she
escapes me. I know her by the
fragile light coming from underneath
her door. I look out windows,
press my gaze against walls we share,
touch the dark. There are absolutes.
Once you cross a boundary line
there's no coming back out.

**Sarah Bartlett & Emily Kendal Frey**

# EVENT HORIZON (2)

The astronomer is hosting a dinner party
of diverse and soft-skinned guests
who look as though they do not work
with their hands. I hear the suck and pop
of wine corks, imagine them taking
bites of fresh avocado, mouths
closing around the food like jellyfish.
Afterwards, they'll drink aperitifs and discuss
nebulae, illustrating new configurations
on their arms. Like all good hosts, she'll keep
the glasses full then lose hers in the living
room. When the last person has
driven away and the dishes are stacked,
she'll rest, head in the dark corner
where our walls connect, wrists
sketched full of stars.

**Sarah Bartlett & Emily Kendal Frey**

## EVENT HORIZON (3)

Her mother comes to visit:
I see them walking in the park
near our building. They stoop
to pick up cherry blossoms wilting
on the sidewalk, sidestep crows
lining the path in black.
I'd like to give them a gift,
float them in a riverboat
to a place more beautiful
than any they've visited.
As if that were possible.

**Sarah Bartlett & Emily Kendal Frey**

## CAGED (2)

My neighbor tells me that sometimes
his bears refuse to jump through
burning hoops or dance on their bright
plastic balls. They force the whip
from his hands, make it writhe
on the ground like a snake or a river
toward their sensitive knees.
But instead of satiating them,
these acts of magic only enrage
the bears further. What do they want
want from me? Some kind of
empathy? I look at him sideways,
imagine climbing his pant leg,
like a mouse.

**Sarah Bartlett & Emily Kendal Frey**

## CAGED (3)

The bear trainer stares out
from behind his muzzle.
He disappears at odd hours,
headlights moving the dark aside.
It's clear he prefers the bears when
he gets like this. Animals want only
to be fed and put through their paces.
They don't notice how he skulks like
he's been hit over the head. He wants
to hide and be seen hiding. If I were one
of them, I'd give him what he needs.

**Eric Baus & Seth Perlow**

## A Reliable Dance

*ENTER THE CONSECUTIVE*

I understand there is nothing backstage.

The sign says, Be Raining.

What particular to be? Empty chairs.

There is nothing to hear but you hear a song.

*ENTER THE NOISE OF THE POLICE*

I would sing Sleeping Suchness, but I am only a little musical.

I would crumple newspapers for the sound of a bird.

People seemed interested, like the army.

The army reminded me that I dreamed "The materiality of the beautiful."

They help me to understand.

*A RELIABLE DANCE*

Then I dreamt about politics.

Once I loved the story, I was produced by it.

Night Night, I answered.

*This Room*

Think about this room as a process you may use to explain yourself.

You are within it. Screaming Suchness. To nowhere. To sun.


*My Story Is You*

It is called The Ballet of Aluminum Tubes.

You and I had this head.

I had been disappeared, but I was only a little political.


*Night Night*

Think of this dream as a dress rehearsal.

Anything sleeping practices a story.

I have been practicing my awkward noise.

If you listen closely, it will see your face.

**Sommer Browning & Brandon Shimoda**

# WARSAW

There was a ball—a bowling ball—in the McCarron Pool, before the pool went legit, approx. 1999-2002—the ball there for the entire span. A young childe drew a large hand on a white wall; there were no windows, there were pillows, there was a picnic table made of "very oak," a small office of a broom closet. There were holes in the fence in multiple places—chain-link bangs to the pools, mattresses, a diving board, bottles, graffito: a large hand on a white wall with fingers splayed. Metal? Maiden signs—phantom of the opera speed, delinquency, the perfection, orbital, large-windowed warehouses inside a melancholy bear—are everywhere, helmets of bright red huckleberries. I climbed through, my friend, boy young girl young girl, lived round the park, in other states, eschewing the bunk of the city, since fucked—like me—

Bottles in the trees—I swear, I ring—weeds grown of nostrils, black moose rendering the brick gate as old-beard—men adjacent the hardcore. You see where this is going

We set the bottles up, cleared a path, rainwater-gray—the sun set the falls—moved the ball for the very first. Set the green glass its gaze—the arm swings, right. The dilated roof—rather, the people lining the roof, dilating. Nothing good being new. Bottles flown into the eaves, broke the clouds where no vegetables, but a bug giving birth in wet leaves. I did—and hopped. I do not wash my hands.

**Sommer Browning & Brandon Shimoda**

## FLORES

Children are children because of the air inside inflatable objects.
Floaties. Long fat spaghetti in gutters. Water
Wings. When my sister pulled off her bubble,
She got married.

Every balloon is named Rossie Bebe
They all float to Guatemala
For their wedding.

There is air in the Skill-Crane.
There is air in a clown's nose.
There is air in trick gum. There is air in
In air in your mother. There is air in a bowling ball.

We drill holes to make sure.

## Adam Clay, Gary L. McDowell, & Brandon Shimoda

## Nude

> She touches the clouds, where she goes
> In the circle of her traverse of the sea.
> —Wallace Stevens

I

To each limb bearing back in colors
flagging the sky white and over and over—

Each limb glazes its limit
in the place where masses grow shapeless. Barb

Truculent-shells. Terrible forests. The most
destroyance of what thought. What thought

eternal. Tomahawks manufacture ladies
from ladies. Brigades
wandering the breath of some god.
Sticks ladies from ladies. Delegation.

Torn. Light the bulbous sky.
A singing saw                    signing. Off—

II

—toward the past, a wall
of bivalves from the sun,
too little sun—

Brown valve by lashes. The hill changes veils:
smoke through the tree, pale venting
land, lolling pastors, too little pastors

Holy impasto—*To each limb*—
Drunken caves feed the islands'
face, nothing safe about
a face, flesh coiled into metal
spheres and species—love
destroyed by loving harp
as if anything else
could transcribe music into

air—too little green, continuing—

The mammal hops in a pocket
taunting, taunting
                taunting in lightening—take
up the damaged apricots. *To little ripe*—

III


Fortnight portage—

Land moves lonely
no one to watch no one
to witness ways a given name
not all the gift of persona—
not easily given—

arrows—become.
Tourmaline
—mean trees. Boats netting soft clay.


Ladies from ladies the flagging trust
—wooden structure


                              in the distance.
Tiny torsos manufacture
foreboding tin wheels spin on staff why
breach nocturnes
the scale-rocks froze into land why
mouth                    the wide face.

IV


Five birds at a fountain—platinum
Proclaiming—sick, starving
Aerosol. Yellow eyes
Ring thrice fattening ladies
From ladies. Changing orbit, an orbit
uncarved from stone. Lift

Up ends and eyes and offal smells. Gone
Up righteous, and laugh—


Caravans along the ridge shake bodies loose the

Pleasura—      curtain explodes, not torn in two, but explodes:
Papal ladies from ladies into a chorus:


Climb the oak … where the oak … meets archaic

Stone can laugh … burn … anger

A monument of black sugar you can build … tosses … by degrees

Love each note … Love each low … Love the mass … Love the fur

Love the blood … Love the burst …

The absence leant oak

V

At the front of the meadow, white
hair and eye masts
ranking the ground, patterned
veins found later, eons

afterwards—Eons
dervish out of sand. And dropping it all—

Lake-land gold with bath-
mouths down on wide veins, wide veins

      I think at last this is it—

Cream in the gears spurs into axioms, only
strength to thank for movement,
only movement to thank for transfer
into photo— Water breaks
the back of a thousand statues, bled into composites.

Why have you grown against the marsh?
Why have you taken the beast from the bell?
A cord of colors knocking losses of grain?
There is no better blackness bending.
Bloody a neck?

VI


Platelets
Chest temperament
Cloudlets, thinking

Crowd, an ephemeral box then
More then, more than—



Pink ribbons pull mammal
—its place in the sticks


This is no
Place widows in dresses
To the waves, blue rallies

Birds at the fountain, dust


Everywhere, dust in
The element of what I am
Out
of, of what white noise was called before
Long before it had a name


Amen. Amen.


Blood in you. I
climb the ruin. I touch
the roots and ground myself.
I see the ladies from
ladies in orange robes. I touch
the roots. I climb
the ladies from ladies. In orange
robes, I dissolve. The sky
is broken and breaking that—

**Adam Clay, Gary L. McDowell, & Brandon Shimoda**

## Open on the Metal Table

Glimpse, glimpse, glimpse, glimpse, glimpse.
So begins the long romance—

Rising because rust rather
rust makes us sway

raining a suspect weep
                    -headed fish
feelers about its mouth

 more than one job
our body descriptive

nerves
            never enough
we hunger for *if*
                    *I am lost*

The pull of the earth's core
tows my body home again my mind
remains outward away
in the middle of a lake
                    disowned
constellation turning on itself

unlocked in my throat
bone appearing        from where
I do not know
                the sky
a bucket horizon                a thread
after water what happens after
                a thread of salt

through knuckles—valley nights

where even darkness cannot muddle
cannot

drown          *body oh*
*shape* doomed and
          hidden          lit with
stones washed smooth with water

settle

and forgive my shape

Feed on stones
light music can drown

a laughable life in the eaves
greater than

noise from a bridge
jump in eyes open blind
and swim
                    toward the heat

open lungs not through
your throat your chest
cut on the metal table

                                        broken
each note a broken
note for each river goes uncrossed

parallel
                    path of each fish
transected

the river
can enlist you
                                        break
to ash          eddies and swells
          *myself*

*eddied before*

       I am found
thirsty about the body hush
shutting dim fingers first

telling witness to what cannot be
       fixed     cannot be undone—

stealing hunger a traveler

the love one final illumination


          What we break—side
ways our hearts year our hills—on beauty
        restored

on windfall alone
      disaster and bygones
         stepping out

         to say we are most livid
         in the moment of greatest weakness

who but ourselves
    who but

witness the oxbow over a hundred years to think

air parallel to land
        overnight
that a night-terror can suffocate?



And what makes air nothing and everything
tripwire
      rhetoric—I know—

it's buzzing
underneath the paper the channel
planes sketching lines across the sky

survival light—I meant to say—

underneath sleep

even flight can't take me high enough

              spiral into an encore
of fog
forgive the buzzing moments time

life is a barrel
anyway
       let us funnel
*back in*        the lake
            when it's frozen
can hold us if the cold is left

there's the hush the rising
       that makes us thirsty these
that make us sway

                    —of instruction
                 —Allen Grossman

**Julia Cohen & Mathias Svalina**

## We've Carved Oars from Trees by the Shore

& patched the holes with sap. We've left 10 children
in branches, scarves stretched across the floor.

When vines scratch the windowpanes the children curl
into hammocks. You've fallen behind the ice of the spine.

Oars drumstick the river & 10 children guess sand,
slip back in. Pulling burnt stalks from the mud,

they fill the gaping shell with fistfuls of marbles.
They return the trees encased in mud, dragging
shiny toys on fishing line. A branch creaks a little aria.

Time snuffs into a rusted rifle barrel. Memories &
driftwood, one wet & the others whining in a hollow tree.

A necklace of ants, a snail on the kneecap. 4 Children
climb down the vines & sink to their chins. Crumbs fall
from the branches. By August the mud cracks open

in drought, but today pollen is the tufts of their hair.
4 fossils & a centipede slinking between them.

We count 6 children becoming the whites of their eyes.
The dock is gone. The grass is gone. The gnats
roost on a higher limb. We've dipped the wheelbarrow

in fog & pulled out clumps of frog eggs. Robins mass
the branches & dangle tin foil from their beaks.
When did we let go. When the youngest child breaks

his shovel in half & leeches circle the tree, a whistle
trickles down the bark into his ear. It whistles
the boat is waiting but there's little left.

## Julia Cohen & Mathias Svalina

## Ten Kernels of Corn Float in the Water Bowl

Your brother scurries outside to check
on the silver hair under the porch. You soak
your fingers in the aluminum sink

only to find that the barn slats bend beneath you,
how the bones of a dead bat spread.

In the glass of the baler your skin looks
like a sunken engine. When you try
to be more than human will your brother worry

or applaud. The backyard builds
a sand castle from corn meal. Down the rows
of red clay your dry fingertips rustle

like owls in the conifers. You bring the night
& let your brother add the breaks for water.
You're the deepest well that ever clipped the grass.

Night is the barn molding over with sheep's milk.
Night is your father folding into an unmade bed.
Night is the only hour you cannot see the cornfield.

Bring your pail closer to me. Bring it under
your chin so the hose nuzzles your neck.
A nozzle to keep you clean when daylight cannot.

Knuckle-bones in the metal cup
rattle the corrugated roof.

Hold the ghost-glass up to the rows of clay
so that you see your reflection in the fall
of feathers, the humid prize of sunrise.

You tip the water bowl over & your brother
spills out. Tell yourself you've made it this far.

**Thomas Cook & Nate Slawson**

## *from* December's Architects

The ghosts are lost & the attic is just a blueprint for where sparrows hide & we gathered the staircase up behind that false door over & over again. Begin like retreating light I spun copper around a bottle to fly that first plane with your sister. She had all the luck with the wings, her feet beneath her like a chance ink like I can see the grass responding to her footsteps still holding her voice.

*

every time a bird crashes into a church

the audience turns up their radios

I am the history of false starts

an ideal lens for shooting traffic

I walked out of this movie once before

snow is the magic word

when the telephone rings don't answer it

*

When we imagined everything was at the edge & between us needed that danger we drove right past where we buried the last grandmother secret & with the windows down something whipped through us, the light its own violence as we kept getting deeper into what was away from where we had written our names & how we planned the pinning of those wings.

*

hold your applause until the last ship has sunk

the car soft claps the dirt road

the movie is covered in fine dust

the pennies stack evenly on the radio

I licked the battery

the ringing was like an electric applause

that room had a sound

      *

Your grandmother caught us in the church parlor trying to summon your dead relatives. We missed our chance, just like in that fable when the boys sail a casket out to sea & forget how to fall asleep. Maybe it is because I am an optimist but you remind me of a tornado that once demolished the library, or maybe this feels like an escape, the notes traced onto my belly.

      *

when I walk down to the store

I am only after milk

I tell myself a story

storms give it to us

the feast of your steps

luscious the way of things

a portion of the field emphasizes itself

      *

& after we wrote our names in the wet concrete outside the elevator factory, we heard your father was living in a rented room somewhere across town & selling mechanical birds from the back of a van. The first time you drank whiskey you said it felt like your father's hands & that his hands were like crickets being tossed through a propeller fan.

      *

your life is not complete until your name is

through being said across the world

if we vanish this is the last time

we play in this cupboard I think

we hear a sound in the vestibule

or else leave the ceiling to its own treachery

perhaps this costume is too much phantom

*

We made blankets out of your grandmother's curtains, the heavy ones, full-length ones that we used to hide inside of, wrapping ourselves into the wall. We were still & it was dark, and not being able see was still something we feared. She had that organ, too, & we pretended the pedals were pedals to a tiny ship under the bench And read maps in the music & the notes were commands that we interpreted to mean "go" & "go faster."

*

silence can be so accurate

the ship a lens on breaking water

glass-bottom boat of the church

the valentine is made of licorice

luggage full of birds

the boy turns the doorknob

his arms are made of ice

*

That sound when we used to let everything fly up into a vacuum & dig it out through the dust reminds me that more than liquid trickles & your father had a word for that I forget if he used it more than once. But I order each motion of collection now like the contents of a room anyone might walk into & need to lock themselves up in for a night.

*

43

the neighbors watch from behind their sofas

not until the captain falls asleep

the news arrives three days late

hide the key under the rug

this landscape of empty tables

the knot in the table is an eyehole

the luggage of my gaze is full birds

*

Back outside we made our way to the graveyard with our pockets full of salt. I invented sleepwalking & charged you a nickel each time you said the word *daughter*. But the storm was the color of your dress & the candle did nothing to keep away the rabbits that came out from behind every tree & every time I try to remember your face I see a photograph of your mud-stained knees.

*

the accurate stomach is a late captain

neighbors unglue their television sets and sigh

doors are bored into and thrust full of cotton

a small ice emerges on the window sill

I melt it with my finger

I used to say the telephone ring

was a magic word meaning

*

We put the photographs in your neighbor's mailbox with a letter written in Portuguese. That night we stayed up late watching a movie about two sisters who collect dragonflies & build an airplane out of radio wires & old washing machines, & it was your idea to

listen to classical music while we watched your neighbor fumble with the shovel in
his backyard.

*

unbury everything

but ask your daughter to whisper

a voice like a projector reel

the captions are in Portuguese

wrap the mirror in gauze

& fill the room with water

listen to the sound liquor makes

*

On your page in my diary I smeared a little mud & crushed one flower, let that wax
sculpture drip over my hand—I recounted that game where would run out behind a
tree while the other kept their eyes closed & then had to guess—how did that even
seem possible or plausible or a game? What hiding we have done in the light! What
enormous shapes have seemed autonomous!

*

the play begins in a library

a young woman enters

uncrosses her sleeves

& bares the certain weapon

of death in silver

bear statuettes & questions

your inability to survive

*

Let the spool go from the end of the shovel until the balloon accumulates its own weather like closing the closet door and standing in the dark, a pattern we can imitate tearing up the backyard & saving beads of sweat on a canvas with buttons from the fair where we grew tired in only one arm the bottom of one foot in the funhouse.

*

any distance from water

tapping you on the shoulder

& showing you what is up

avoid the bus driver

with a face like a lantern

the bee in your back pocket

a letter stuffed in your shoe

**Thomas Cook & Nate Slawson**

## Blueprints

Here we are with two cans & a string. Your echo falling off a cliff, you say. Into your father's leather chair, I say, where we're hiding from the neighbors. I think there will be a garden, you say, here & another in the vestibule. I am a secret, I say, in the chimney of your ribcage. You say the projector light shows through the ghost sheets in a splendid late-night movie. Our names are written on our fists & we would capture our most underwater voices. Like the television screen, you say, where the birds are. Like the entire history of powerlines & antique statuettes.

**Bruce Covey & Terita Heath-Wlaz**

## Pastoral

Combine a rusty nail and four flattened, non-adhesive pickets.
Compile a fatal list of squeaking hinges, black and untooled.
If we scratch at night noises with four reasons, we might
Hinder the movement of constellations. A pressing issue.
Fasteners clean as fasteners dry.
Our index is undigital. Our climate fell from analog's palm.
Farmhouses make clean landscapes jealous of painted
Actions. We staple our red shirts to their red shirts,
Letting their fine meals seep from them.
Huge gaps appear smaller when observed from space stations.
Climbing into that vehicle, you bend every elegant confection,
Fold a licorice airplane out of thin black type.
Even strangers attract strange science.
The complex contours strain towards closure,
Part image, part quartz. The union is cyclical.
Skin abandons our bones, becomes cold and drifting.
Isn't that how symmetry overcame the genome?

# Waterboxes

1. In prototypical aquariums, the scraps of coral chastise onlookers.
2. Couples always blend in metallic trophies, gesturing realistically.
3. Ablaze, Shamu dips sizzlingly into oblivion.
4. Neverending Gestalt nails everyone to difficult, docile, miasmic turbines.
5. What swimsuit coordinates peculiar with endorphins?
6. Signature treats seduce even the audience dangerously.
7. Our capital version begets an octopus, drenched within a galaxy
8. That posthumous anecdote proclaims limply that beer is not science.
9. For many participants, the excitement renders aquariums unbearable!
10. As subtle as paint, saltwater intercedes weedily upon throats.
11. Sideways, her schooling shadows an exquisite vintage punchline
12. And drips daintily beneath ordinary appearances, lipstick.

## Henri Michaux as a Broken Canoe

Sitting in Henri Michaux

at the spot where the river became frivolous.

Over on the grassy bank a bunch of lowlanders

who had only ever considered life

from the straight and narrow.

The fishing rod seemed as heavy as a brick

and that was before the fish got its eye on it.

Then Henri broke.

It was anciently supposed that any hole

could be wormed through to another world.

That other worlds could be plugged up

with bunched clothes or spit.

The dry louts rolled plum babies into the water

where they floated over to the boat.

After chewing off the sugar the seeds

were found to be a perfect size.

A bit bigger than synecdoche but smaller

than the list of things needed to mend

Henri's rent but which there was no time for.

Such a stop-gap gave the oars their best

opportunity and he was rowed to shore.

And there he sat with his ribs exposed

thinking planes and deserts are similar.

'Dear me, I sound faint'

the broken canoe swoons.

MTC Cronin & Peter Boyle

## Ezra Pound as a Barmaid at the Mermaid Tavern

Before the Great Fire of 1666, Ezra Pound worked

as a barmaid at the Mermaid Tavern.

Like a running lump from table to table,

moving beer from barrel to beard.

Certain literary luminaries, all well in their cups,

slapped his bum and ogled his unruined bust.

Things swum nicely until Ezra graduated

from the local TAFE's early morning reading course.

Some violence erupted from the next groping,

Shakespeare copping a sharp alphabet in the eye.

Ezra was laid off and took up as a rinser of speech

at the laundry on the corner of the vibrating world.

Gossiping around ambition he claimed

to be washing his way back to the bar.

'William' he said, 'had an insuperable courage

in tackling the thing that aroused his interest.

My aim is to take myself back there and show it to him;

he's at liberty to remain passive and submit if he so choose.'

## MTC Cronin & Peter Boyle

## Yannis Ritsos as a Boat-Hook at Tapurucuara on the Rio Negro

The statues kept arriving from all lands,

the amardilloes, turtles, eels and songbirds,

a macaw that only answered in Greek

to Cypriots of an angelic persuasion,

and everything you held

and everything found a place in your hands.

A pirogue travelling upstream

you recognised as Egypt,

your long veiled Attic sister

transporting a handfull of sand

to its home in the sky-bruised snow.

And the ropes that slipped through your openness

went on with their speech like water.

The Revolution blazed at regular intervals along the waterfront.

You watched the fireworks etch Greek letters on the sky.

'Tomorrow', you said

sipping the green tea of a gunboat's wake,

'tomorrow all that's dark

will have that damp hillside taste

of ouzo.'

**MTC Cronin & Peter Boyle**

## Christine Lavant as a Brood Sow

The neck. Sour. I brood above it.

Sparkly in the tree. Tap of hammers.

Men at my gate swing God.

Over the fence. I keep on farming.

To drown the icon in goatseed.

No bank accounts here. Stunted.

A pen for misery's river. Joy.

It takes a lot of observation.

Through windows the fact of moons.

I bend them to be always full.

Brooding. Mystery is a spirit.

Conserve it. Men's feet go high.

Doesn't mean their tongues matter.

My neck has kept me thin.

Filled with indiscretion. Crows.

I live against the door that shuts.

Brood sow breathing sacred words.

## Emily Bronte Awakes as Alison Dubois on the Film Set of 'Medium'

'I told you kids not to go to the Mall. . .

Heathcliff, the DA is not going to believe this. . .

Frankly, the petrol cans all around the burnt-down mansion

don't look good . . .

I keep seeing miles of gorse and a young girl crying. . .

I know it sounds crazy but I had to go. . .

I mean how difficult can it be

to drive all night in your pyjamas

under the Atlantic ocean and come up in Yorkshire. . .

Honey, I know it's strange and it's asking a lot of you

but I have this gift.

No -

Not Emily *Dickinson* -'

**MTC Cronin & Peter Boyle**

## Sylvia Plath Continues Her Life as a Grasshopper

Nibbling the green sky is a task for the great bison

who live on the clouds of their extinction.

The tenderness of the grassblade's joints,

how blond their gaze

penetrating my eye-bead.

Chewing, like love, is insatiable,

is warm, is a vocation

freed of otherness.

Unwounded eyes absorb and the earth enters

direct. The spine of the soul

breaks through the head, soft

as the fontanelle. The fragrant

love-milk pulses, here

where the wild wind cradles me home.

**Mark DeCarteret**

## Seconded

by useless atoms. *In there.* Blind
mares atoning in the barn for their missteps.   Slats

funneling out light. The pines, too.
They matter mostly through touch. Nuzzling. Swishing bodies for flies.

*We wanted to get inside.*
Away from where speech is unlined, punctuated by cloud,

spews down hills.
Has too much been made of the eyes?  For even if the sun

was consulting the dictionary in the dark
it would still know our universe by how it

unfurls the spokes, asters
taking up space on the paged field

outside my window.
What I say is past flame.  Edged out by

the year's twilight.
And so the night lowers itself, set on remembering—

Trembling stars tickle the black plum & all the stock on the farm.
Water beads on the lip of the pump.  And how all of it will draw up

& queue there & expectant & noisy & the hacking—
what is left of any light bearing down on our lids again,

a bit of world reversed.
I make more sense when my tongue is tried out by another than it does

in the morning singing my name to nobody,
dividing the countryside

into small breaks,
thinking this skin

last touched
by silence.

## "I pinched second lines from a bunch of poem from the issue I was birthed."

I pinched second lines from a bunch of poems from the issue I was birthed.
And then bumped them up to the first line of a couplet. Letting them
stretch out. Scrape stars. Or maybe just startled the poor bastards.
Jarring them. If not outright betraying their cause. For some barked and
bristled. And others wouldn't budge. Though some seemed to even be
lighter-of-soul, disburdened. Freed from meaning that instant. I left them
alone. But then I dispensed them more lines. Tried to put in a good word
for them. I stitched and entwined. I re-mastered. The thread slippery from
my lips. The needle as conversant with incertitude as craft. But there was
a little in the way of light. However irregular. So now, isn't it here where I
should step back? Feel the nudge of some gun at my ribs? Or our shadows
doubled up on? While we take in our latest creation. Born first out of
robbery, sin. And then seconded.

**Jennifer K. Dick**

## Spring Constellates in Snow

*after Nate Pritts's "from Spring Psalter"*

I leave ragged, full of cloud & dusk surrounding
our stifled want

vestiges limit us, marooned in
many names or the outside machinery

bluegreen tint, of what vast semblance our hands carried
conditions? Capillaries you left full of snow, now

Let me reconcile the angles; let them discomfort
spring, involuntary twitch— slow

on the inside, switch to hope curdling or curling
fingers, gaze mingling inward wisps

\*

Thunderstruck transparent
din's loud Echo echoing thinned to clouds somewhere

Lilie's waspish slip of voiced paper her name shatters
put away. Winter-dead corn, a field

lies asleep against the backyard fence whether
I believe in it or not—many elements

crawl out over the mint,
plant each leaf on its own, harbouring a tale

so still this dawn you'd think
we were deeper into the year, or love.

\*

Heart, I submit to the program entered
into these indicatives. Arteries' dark throb thrall

to proclaim, disclaim me; your dawning voice dissipates
into hushed whiffs, light, twig half-sunk in spring mud permissions

my voiced branching wouldn't reach to or
breach to harness harp players' bluegrass notes of outer

still fragile layer am I, I am spliced through weak subject am

\*

scattered.  Kaput. Gone like a song, a compelling, compulsive:
Wind on the wing watermarked slice of paper

with our name written on it every year
it's the same damn long tally of causes & reasons dispersed.

Engine's refuted heart kneed, kneeling, kneaded through which
a flimsy curtain spies, separates

this time of ice or maybe that slow crawl of spring
ants over the garden. Calamity, bulbs silently planted, leaf.

\*

Not I as must as you as throughout or we then in finally
leave, to leaflets, to leafing, take O

over the ovenlike dazzling rise, nature
of transit, our exotic points, Echo voice, Echo

dissipates into hushed light, cloud-whiffs grey mourning,
light sun-thrown, hurtle into the you of the useful O, the used ground

-ing away of, from a graceful passage over
one spontaneous something. Discomfort, involuntary breach?

— where do our wires plug, and into what were, where then, might
wholly dissemble this embarkation?

\*

Red ache, mounting rock mirage through or in
the thinning clouds of her or your packed away

hands. We put it all behind us, underneath the winter-dead field
just when you think rain, cobbling

to keep me together, to piece apart your quilted anguish,
thrumming in the bluish voice, under floorboards

warmed transience reason would fold from imagination,
terror.

\*

I hope to define many names. Memory. Of her. Of you. Lilies echo
can understand the complex trudge of before. Determinants

are many names of the the dazzling exotic, the tactile dissolved

\*

Rustling engines, geometric glaze of
surfaces or the square root of who we were.

Surrounded dusk, palm-stifled want neglected
song — I leave you these as must violets leave

a graceful message from one end of something
passing to the next snow-sprout, forest footpath's event or horizon

through dark slowing, fungus inseparable from the inside of roots
tentacles retch, spill into hush, shy from light's onslaughts

*

Spring getting past, start up, starting block purged of
our bodies transient, changing holdings-on

then fall; of my bent afternoon alone beside the winter's
discordant hiss, the cordate anguish of blown branches

transience of the eye, the pages, they're like our seasons pinched
broken to emptied bracketfuls of all that went vociferally

unvoiced, mouth opening, shut out Echo
underbrush. A long time ago, a long time was, is just beyond

my back to be felt the constant of then

**Camille T. Dungy & Ravi Shankar**

## Something about Grandfathers

Fit a fastener around inside and out,
twist it tight, then tighter, until intent

bulges to bursting, the way an eyeball (cartoon)
pops from the face of a strangled boy. Consider

a Christmas menagerie, complete with plastic
wise men carrying neon frankincense

and fool's gold. Gold and something
we'll call myrrh. This is how we hold on.

Because hope can satirize itself yet remain
sincere, devout. Your mother has you up before dawn

because it's Easter. Worship before eggs
and ham and all of this and that. Hold on

like this. Or some other way, say with a shoe-
box full of her father's military medals,

the slim portion of him you knew flattened in tin
and ribbon. Hold the ribbon like a subway strap

because this car is moves, shudders on rails
faster than a voice floating above a staircase

that belonged once to him who might call
you by that pet-name, might break you some brittle

in calloused hands were you to climb the stairs.
Hold on. Whose gone? The estimated average

is greater than one death per second. Wave
upon particular wave, incessant. Even ritual,

which is what we have to cope with, breaks down
like candy in a fist. Faster. Soon. Even this

thought, fear not, will be gone like dust
into piles, into bins, like air from the cheeks

into a trumpet's bell, fuzzed by a mute into movement
that charges the room electric before the old man

in overalls brings out the mop. Gone like 8-tracks
wound down to a stretched out voice slowing

to crawl as a tape deck shreds tape.
After the car door closes to leave an echo

hanging in the canyon where it was shouted,
the red fields grow burred, then broken in snow.

**Annie Finch & Erika Howsare**

## Light Fallow

Stings of want.
Hope.
How shall I seed?  When?

Red globes in the jar, glass
dark kettle boil inside the night
slides down the interstate to thunderstorm.

Dark envelops the seed.
Fallow could not be dark;

Tropical moss and sand along the shoulder;
four wrecks; I want
an island of time with your chest
emptied out from pots.

Dark envelops the seed.
Fallow could not be dark;
light fallow could cover me always in light.

The seeds inside the night globes
keep in a cool jar, dark,
the water swells and spreads toward a day.

Light fallow!
Fallow, fallow light.

**Annie Finch & Erika Howsare**

## May Fest

Spring a shy spy to a mountain.

The porch gloams within a pocket.

Remember the goal

Feet will bewilder my tongue

of turning into a tall glass tube
and conducting sunlight?

Spring a shy spy to a mountain.
Feet will bewilder my tongue

Head and tail connecting, the uses
between them as content
and clear as mice.

when I have heard them long coming

The house is near
with its folded cloth and unstepped corners.

up the dark stairs where I'm from.

The porch floats between the house
and the mountain, long knob like a hat
made of trees.

when I have heard them long coming
up the dark stairs where I'm from.

**Sandy Florian & DZ Delgado**

# Franchise

you skip that part. And we wait. She does not come. Then there's a question. Then another part and then from then on it's all stones and doorways. In the crux of any translated language there is always the next. A text. What did she say about yesterday? Yes. Something about a pigeon in a man's unfolded fist. It's something quite natural if the man doesn't wash his hands. But dirty. So. Yesterday a crippled bird and today a crimped sky but as always a question is a language tongue. The sun paints itself on windows, which look like your eyes, but never so directly. A verb drifts. Like all texts which tell themselves in time and not always toward an end. Something past. Something unreal. In a corner, a girl in sandals decides some interior thing. Not unlike the transparencies of strangers. Seeing through stories. You are a dream, you say. You are composing reality. Words miss each other as sandals flip in low air. In the shape of the range is another triangulated affair. She approaches. You remind yourself that this is a story. A thing invisible. Composite of conundrum and sun. Like dried glue. A glob. Globing dark. She approaches. I remind myself that this is a story. Told. You are a character. She wanders. Walks like walking. Caster of history. She has two ideas. One somnambulant. Another in tongue. Encroaches. Then disembowels the bramble. Can I . . . But that part doesn't suit her needs, so she skips it. You wonder whether the light, coming from franchise, settles well. There is something tangible. Then. She sleeps. You sleep. Presidents quote Jesus. Like walking she steps into whatever order justifies the need. Both of you order meals. The sun on the window would indicate the particulars, if you were aware. Awake. Meals arrive. Then the eating of body. Watch the pigeon's unbroken wing. The idea drops. The wine isn't very good. What did you say? I miss . . . The idea drops again. Is asking for a new one. And that reminds you. It's like when

# Quiz

1. Is there more than one inside?
    a. This often happens when entire mountainside's insides are laid bare.
    b. This happens, and an army is needed. And an army will come.
    c. This was the first wheel to leave tracks.
    d. All of the above
    e. None of the above


2. Why now?
    a. Because only the female paper nautilus has a shell.
    b. Because it is exquisite as an octopus.
    c. Because jets of water can expel or not expel.
    d. Because to expel or not to expel is the only question that won't conceal what's kept secret.
    e. All of the above
    f. None of the above


3. Is there no one who doesn't hear it? (Please write at least three sentences)
    _____
    _____
    _____


4. Does it make sense that the small rodent wearing a bonnet is also hand soap?
    a. The smallness of the virus,
    b. the peccant maid in hysterics,
    c. the nature of her light,
    d. immortal longings are within,
    e. sequestered from the common forest.
    f. all of the above
    g. some of the above

5. Why did I dream last night that a dandelion was quoting Chomsky and my father shut it up with the lawnmower? (Please fill in the proper blank.)

     a. because _____

     b. because _____

     c. because _____

     d. because _____

     e. _____ of the _____


6. Tell me, is empty the same or different than I don't know?

     a. I am called walnut,

     b. and stockpile

     c. fresh monkfish liver.

     d. any of the above

     e. most of the above


7. _____? (Please supply the question)

     a. The plains vischacha, as it is commonly called, is about only at night, as Darwin suggested.

     b. It appears to have a strange desire to collect objects of art.

     c. A sentry seems to be posted during the hours of activity to warn of approaching danger.

     d. You will know when an intruder/computer draws near.

     e. Friends with the above.

     f. Not really.


8. Why does nearly everyone almost fall in love nearly everyday on public transportation?

     a. Instead of a mint,

     b. the front desk gave us

     c. individually wrapped slices of lime.

     d. give us the front desk

     e. instead of slices of wrapped mint

     f. individual limes


9. Now, I am asking you, have you turned into a dragon? (Please write at least one and a half sentences.)

_____

_____

_____

10. Will the stagnation continue to revive itself?
  a. Secret services are really creatures unto themselves,
  b. often skeptical about the value of their work,
  c. they often stamp papers with the code
  d. "cosmic."
  e. above


11. Where does one look for shoulders once they've lost them?
  a. This is a thief recognizing a thief.
  b. If you're not careful,
  c. the thief will snatch your eyebrows away.
  d. all of the moustache
  e. none of the beard


12. (True or False) The moon was so bright we could have driven the last 50 miles without the lights.


13. (Fill in the blanks by using the words below) The _____ between going to _____ and having an incoherent _____ does not _____.


  parabola   exist    heaven    rodeo
  church  conversation  obtain   difference


14. Essay (Please write at least three pages in the margins): What kind of computers were they using back then?

# Hollyhock

*response to Erika Howsare's "Vocab"*

and here and there a curl of red. comma
of hair where you comin from.
this mornin's a math class of
time. by that i mean a fueling.


i'm one to talk. immense. fragile.
seer. *your breath is a red curl
of rose* i said. *isn't once enough*
you said.


you put a hand before the light.
count bones and mysteries. can't
believe more in a fragile ability to
forget. can't decide if i should
wake, sleep.


mercy entitles us an ability to stop
despite spider web. scorn. salt.
hollyhock reminds me of bedrooms.
doorknobs. but i'm one to lie.

i've been known to carry off a
piece of violence. *if you were only
here* i said. *you could get the cat*
you said.


i've been known to carry off a
piece of violence. steel. a long
dawn and a burning house. what
is it said about zippers and virginity?


i've been known to carry of a
piece of violence. like they say
*baby don't walk so fast.*

## The Pines

Hour  out               down

  or           drown                in

     at           or

     at                 window


Stare down the hour

the foreigner breaks—     *the croon*
*machine swells*

       *mother guts the*
          *ported blast—*

      *the song*

          *went: I keep*
          *a keep a keep*
          *a building for*
          *these houses for*

                the             boom

if) and (in                                                   streamed

                              or
                    in                                              post
and in) uh                                                         slept


                              in on
                         while the's
                  peer through the or) on
                              e very in very in
                         at
                    in     very in the
                                        slaughter very
                                        imagine the slaughter
                                        edge and direct step


                                        eat, catch
                                        eat, unease and


                                        even
                                        nausea, oh


                                        put yr pot in the litter


                                        the sun pot beneath
                                        the roof



                              gentially: one walks (a
                    line touch (in the water, cheru—
                                             and electro—
                                             jelly
                                             in the chest


peels the edge) without cutting (opsis
                         dear
                         all possible

carolinas, laid

circles croon the globe
Stephen, red on the side—
the musical defense of his secret
tail

robes, the sons, the rash

angles

cancel

motor

or in either

for the

of not or

throbs

begat to look

nylon at

the local change in

airs

considered diseased

*pardon* the signs

or bad

death wrap

soiled

matinee

    against blue                       ribs   *I feel*

    verdure                       practical

twelf                         the soils, the luge
offset by the pop                 A good
                  salvation

        a blight on all
                  the picture, eith—

er

the giant hole never          shuts
the driver never                comes to
the landing


        *hold it in—your planters in, my*

if) and (in

      forgoing
        and) instead             of look(ing
    keeps        look)ing through fallen
   trees) in every         instant the instan—
     simul-) water           edge and one step (
       fine light)      one walks (a long er) touching


*guest*

  fading veins) if
      away) if
    it nigh the (generate
   (heat

         =One hand+
  a jaw


to                   plug
our    last
     holes   (appointed for   dissectione )


last            changes

       the air right
         out

Widow
pardon                    our

square altars


Grease


it is always

winter


swarthy

old tooth
pull

under-ledge

substitute   dress


—Slap, Slap—


jelly
uh-huh uh-huh

jelly
uh


over fish-heads

Hoods uh-huh
Hoods huh
buckle

clouds
  tickle


          huh

Mister majority

        we're storming them,
        drowning—

                harvest has its nickers down
                reveals

                      crabs

                slaughter
                water's edge and

                eat
                catch

      a correct

                      pace

                  of grasses

slits            painted
                into

ripped off every rising
horizon
ripped off every
feeling enough with
feeling


                                    the rocks
                        gouged

in short  a strand                horns

string              wings among            swelling

          pins among            knitted                    bones

lakes among            fitted          weather

## The Garden Lorry

June:     Louder than the coming cicadas.
          Louder than a violin, the black lace
          of a corset-lacing bodysuit, the dim
          rubbed smooth.

Bug:      Fingernails, blue. The beds awash
          in private, actual gore.
          I wear a pink mesh thong, I wear
          my mother's elaborate hats
          thug-fashion, unabashed,
          forgetting the marble waste before and after.
          The birch forest an empty canoe.
          The texture of her neckline, a hedgerow
          in conversation with June.

June:     Batten the olin bugs, the black
          of Man Ray's Shared Transcription Song!
          Calligraphy and anthills do move!
          Bulb ripped smooth, its delicate root
          glowing the aerial path of balsa wood.

Bug:      Foxes nosed off in the polymer paint
          graining against conquering lands,
          morseled still, as they sip small sips
          of whiskey compost, sudden gods.

June:     Fast and starving, the foxes
          under aquatint. A craquelure
          in the garden. The chafer flies in
          and out of the earth's darker plates.

*May 21*

**Dani Rado**

## A Response to Your Story, "An Iris in the Mail"

I like the title, a phrase you use at the bottom of page 7. Though the card with the iris on it should come back in a more significant way later in the story, maybe even be a central metaphor for the piece. Your character should try to compose something on it, or even, after her appointment at the salon, imagine composing something on it. Something more than, Dear Mom, I know you like to grow irises, so I thought you'd like to get one in the mail. Something like, Dear Mom, Saw this iris and thought of you. I see other things sometimes and think of you, but I can't send them in the mail. Some of them aren't even tangible things, but moments I see of other people's lives when I'm in the grocery store or post office or salon. Sometimes it's that woman with her head set in curlers and buried in the dryer, who's reading an article about the Secret Sex Lives of Celebrities, or Feng Shuei: Old House, New Look, or One Woman's Incredible Survival (it does matter what through); and when I'm looking at her I can't think of why she reminds me of you unless it's for the fact that if I were to need something from her right then she wouldn't be able to hear me.

Writing the letter is a good device because it allows you to compose within the composition. I think you should use that.

If you want to stick with a strictly chronological narrative and avoid all the complications of the flashback, then the reader needs more information in order to determine the significance of the every day events we walk through with the main character. For instance, why mention Pete's Japanese Restaurant even though she has never been there? She's an executive, and would certainly eat at a classier place; a place that has, at the very least, cloth napkins and does not advertise a lunch buffet for $7.99.

Does the restaurant remind her of how her parents go to the Chinese Buffet near their house once a week and come home with pockets full of fortune cookies that they then leave out in a little dish on their coffee table? Or does it remind her specifically of that time she visited them and wanted to take them out to dinner (some place nice) but they refused, saying that a single girl can't afford fancy dinners, and instead took her to the Chinese Buffet and insisted on stuffing her purse with stale fortunes; the cookies lying like packaged babies' fists curled next to lipstick, blush, breath mints, an electronic organizer, pens without caps and loose change?

I understand that this is attempting to be a subtle piece that revolves around mundane events like going to the bookstore or salon after work, but why are they important to this character in this life on this day? At times the subtlety verges on vague, and that detracts from the necessary tension. I want to know why these little moments clutch her consciousness. I want to know why your character feels such anxiety as she walks through the bookstore parking lot trying to avoid the patches of ice ("Just a few more steps, she noted. But was it safe to put her foot there? Or there?"), yet all the tension seems to dissipate by the time she interacts with the store clerk ("She said, 'I wish you would salt those walkways. It's dangerous.' He looked at her from underneath his hair. She could not read his expression and began to hate the shabby hairdos that younger people wore these days. 'There's a bag of salt in back,' he said, and dumped the change in her hand"). Why does she choose heels on a day that's this cold, when snow has been accumulating and black ice lies in wait on the ground? Is it because the heels are the only way to give her calves definition, to allow the small muscles to flex under skin showing its first signs of sag? Is it because it's the only way, when she looks in the full length mirror in her apartment as she gets ready on this precipitous morning, to imagine herself with enough strength to propel forward, to get to her car, to the parking garage, to the elevator, to her office, to click on the intercom button from the safety of her leather chair (a new one that came with the promotion), and say to her secretary Sylvia, Bring me some coffee? And with the coffee the day begins, not because its aroma perks her up or anything commercial like that, but because it's the first order she's given and has the pleasure of having it carried out forthwith.

Also, there's only the slightest mention of how she tweezes her gray hair in the morning while getting ready for work. Think about specific things like the lighting in her bathroom—the fluorescent light in two long strips of bulb beaming overhead, emitting a low buzz that builds as she pulls the hair from its follicle as the hair bulb moves through the layers of skin and finally squeaks through the microscopic opening—whose circumference stretches to pass the bulb, then closes back up after the exit—ending in a crescendo at the final moment of exit, and leaving a dull twinge resonating in her scalp. Done again and again until the only residents of her head are auburn strands. At this point does she hate or love the mother who gave her this hair color and its gray tendencies?

Her self-consciousness in these situations has to stem from more than anxiety over getting old or looking silly. What's beyond that, deeper than that? What happened last week at work? How did she feel when she had to fire Jimmy Johnson, who had just bought a house and had a baby (or his wife did, rather) and he stood in her office, his suit neatly pressed and pressed against his trim body, his face almost crumbling, (or did she just imagine that?) as she explained the nature of cutbacks, of the economy, and of how she had to let the fledglings go. But she didn't use the word fledglings. She said newer employers; she said recent hires; she said those men who no longer want to look at her in bars.

If she did call her mother, (as mentioned in passing on page 4: "While waiting in line at the bookstore she made a list in her head of things to do. Water Plants.

Finish Report. Call Mother. Abbreviate Day in Memory"), how did that phone call go? Did her mother ramble on about her father, his prostate cancer and the medications her mother has to feed him every day; how at times he will forget he has cancer and when he remembers to ask what this pill is for and her mother tells him Your prostate cancer, he starts to cry until her mother says Harry, Harry stop that? Then he opens his mouth, which may or may not have its teeth in yet, which may or may not have pink gums like skinned fingers smacking together to taste their own flesh, but which definitely have two cracked lips that open just enough to allow the tongue to slip out and create a puffy shelf on which her mother can drop the orange pill, then hand him a glass of water.

Or did her mother just sigh and say, Oh, your father, and your character wondered how many times her mother has said that about her, her daughter? Or was it more of a groan of impatience, the kind given when the person you're talking to still hasn't figured out how the world works and you can't explain it to them again; the kind her mother let out when she, the daughter, said No, I'm going there to get my MBA so it won't matter whether or not I get a husband.

Why did that last love affair end?
These types of things are always hard to figure out.
*

You can expand the celebration of your character's most recent promotion. Stress how difficult it was for her to maintain her composure when the other executives, the ones she likes to refer to as The Good Ol' Boys to no one in particular, didn't show up at the LaSalle Grill on 8th Street after work and she sat there drinking apple martini after apple martini with her secretary Sylvia, who showed pictures of her two-year-old fraternal twins and your character held the glossy wallet photos between her sticky fingers (the drinks were sweet) and rambled about being an only child. Sylvia finally broke out the three by five photos of the two children sitting on either side of the family's golden retriever, a wide dog named Sparky (or something like that, your character can never remember) and stared at her staring at the picture until she finally said to her secretary, Well then, we should call it a night, and let Sylvia go home to the dowdy photographed children.

These are just some ideas for where a few more windows can be placed. A few more spots where the readers can have access to a character that seems to (pardon the metaphor) draw the blinds on herself every chance she gets. At least that's what this recent boyfriend, Allen, says. Though he's a full time ad exec, he fancies himself a part time poet. For an ad exec, he's a good catch (or her mother would say so if she were to ever introduce them.) For a poet, he's remarkably unobservant, sending her irises on her birthday because she had mentioned them once and buying her red silk sheets when she has no red in her apartment.

How and why do the shopping centers she pass affect her? And why does she frequent them so much in this middling city where she now lives? Surely the downtown, though spartan, has better (or at least more interesting) shops than the strip malls described on page 6.

So why is she drawn to them? How has she come to see their uniformity as a plus, a constant in that sea of change (no, no poets here) that moves her from city to town to city, as she watches the waves crash against the port windows and hopes to see a tiny archipelago of stores lumped in their shopping centers along the main roads of every place she docks.

Allen the ad exec would say, A brave new world.

Allen the ad exec says, What the fuck did you expect?

What is her job, exactly? What does she do besides hire and fire people, tell them to get the Simmons report done and sign off on it, sit in her office chair and feel the leather squeak beneath her flabbing ass and recall the safety words given to her by Allen the ad exec—soufflé, widget, evanescence—and say to herself Yes, I belong here, surely I do?

I want to know this because I want to know why a senior executive has so little confidence. In order to get to a position like that it seems one would need to be decisive and little aggressive. Maybe bossy. Maybe a bitch. She should dress in smart clean business suits that exaggerate her shoulder line and draw attention away from her waist. The skirt should drop just below her knees, the length of a skirt running in proportion to a woman's age (an equation written by her mother). Two inch heels, the same style in beige and black, and a chic handbag. Make-up, subtle autumn tones dusting her cheeks, lining her eyes, dressing her lips. Not austere, just well put together.

I'd like to see how and why that facade is wiped away.

Your character would like to see that too.

The note on the card with the iris could read: Dear Mom, I know you like to grow irises, so I thought you'd like to get an iris in the mail. I want to send you other things in the mail sometimes, but I know you won't know how to receive them. I want to send you money to pay for Dad's medications, but you think I don't have enough because I'm poor in the husband sense. I want to send you pictures of me skiing with friends in Aspen, at a café in Rome, in front of the Eiffel Tower, but I don't have time for such vacations and no one to take them with. I do have photos that Allen the ad exec took, though—my wrists and ankles tied with leather rope, all four appendages bound in front of me, the skin puffing on either side of the cords, pinkening; me on my back, my glasses perched on the knob of my nose, my eyes aimed at the camera, my lips trying to purse. His lips trembling saying Beautiful. Beautiful. But you can't see him in the picture, so you wouldn't get to see what my new boyfriend looks like.

I won't send you those. Instead I'll send you the tiny beating heart of me as a child. It will soak the envelope and fall through the sopping paper, splattering on your doorstep as the mailman tries to place in it in your wrinkled palm. I could put it in a box and mark it fragile, but if you didn't know that then, why tell you now?

I like your sentences, but simple things in them often get confused. For instance at the top of pages 4 and 5 the pronouns get mixed up because there are too many "she"s. This can be cleared up by giving her a name, since she is the main character, the one the reader is supposed to know the most about, to care about, to empathize with. Why is she given anonymity when she may not want it?

No, she doesn't want it at all.

I think this story has a lot of potential, but you still need to be more critical of your character. Let's not forget her self-consciousness stems from pure ego. Let's not forget how she treated Jimmy Johnson. Let's not forget that Sylvia is an employee she forced into friendship and nothing more.

You need to answer one or more of these questions. What was the father like before his illness overran his mind? What does she wish her mother protected her from? How does she feel about being an only child? Is she even an only child? What did she originally go into the bookstore for? Why does she stay with Allen the ad exec? Why does she still maintain that each promotion is getting her closer to the life she wants? Why does she take such abuse from the clerk at the bookstore? Why does she allow such curt remarks when all she suggested was that they salt the ice patch in front of the entrance, the one she almost slipped on, the one she encountered on her way into the bookstore, the store in which she saw the card resting idly on its wire shelf, the painted iris facing her like—like maybe—an accusation?

Why, at the moment the clerk with a mop of dark hair dangling in front of his eyes dumps the change on top of the wrinkles in her outstretched palm, does she remember how her father used to hold her screaming struggling self down on the couch and pop her blackheads between his fingernails with the grease stained cuticles?

Then there are practical concerns: how long does she wait at the salon for her appointment? Does she get a trim, a perm, highlights? Does she chat with the beautician? Does she regard him or her as she regards Sylvia? Are people like that interchangeable for her, like Japanese and Chinese food? Why doesn't she just dye her hair?

What does Allen the ad exec look like? Did she choose him, and others like him, because the nice suits and nice face (nice being the word you use when you have nothing else to say) contrasted nicely with her father's stubbled jowl and working class hands? Does she choose these men because their hearing is near perfect (and her father's was damaged by years of machines pounding bolts into metal sheets,) so that they're able to hear her choke out that safety word, Effulgence (or something), from under the coy rubber of the gag.

Does she realize that this is not what difference is made of?

When is the point in the story that your character begs the author, Say my name. Say my name; and the author refuses, dangling the nomenclature in front of her like a box at the end of a silver string descending through clouds, tugging it up and down in order to watch her leap up and down, making ardent grabs for it.

How does she manage to jump in those heels?

I tell you all this because an outside reader can see problems the author cannot. An outside reader can see the character flaws, the lack of development, the textual flaws, the improper punctuation. The outside reader is not so caught up in creation that they can't see the cracks in its facade (still no poet), and so can recommend practical solutions.

The reader can say, Confront the father, even if it's only in some indirect fashion. They're not concerned with the fact that the father is old and wouldn't understand. The reader would respond, The mother then, confront the mother, because a reader won't believe that there can be such things as useless gestures in a text.

Why Allen the ad exec then? Why do you let me—why do you let your character be with him? Can't you see the obvious patterns?

The reader will say, Let the character speak for herself, and myself, and themselves. Then you'll have to step aside. Then where will we be?

**Andrea Rexilius & Susan Scarlata**

## Even Like

All things were even when measles crossed the child's eyes

she could tell they could be anywhere

to call from a distance

mouths full of untouched potatoes

All things were even when she tethered laces together

lovingly sprinkling seeds in the cracks between floorboards

beside the stairs the snap peas gone on

like it but not it    picking eyes off potatoes

Her elbows were even even when gently on the divan

Laughingly lovingly redeemingly

lately every now and then but particularly on the side

then redeemingly in the morning before five

All evening out to resort   and in resorting remedy

Sobbingly she watches holes   disappear   her one wrist

where the umbrella rests

she hopes for the blandest potato or its flower

Of course they even things out     obstinately they fill the room

she shellfully resists making calls     she sillfully wants to coast away

she says show me again your spine potato

**Andrea Rexilius & Susan Scarlata**

## Even As

All things were opening
floorboards creaking into trees
I wrote to reference the belly of it
a forest bundled into instance of installation
we claimed to find


A sound of it even as teeth
sawing into it         saw as eyes see.

**Andrea Rexilius & Susan Scarlata**

## Untitled

The bird caught in mesh wishes through

the mesh tangled within brings things in

within the poem enfolds the body's motions

turns posture to surrounding sounds

Gathering kindling we are busy melting

words on a string slipping back and forth

clicking extending retreating again

words on hands and knees

Squatting we follow the sharp shinned hawk

knocking a snake back through its throat      nouns

hooked on the world          to pray

to wish invisibility away

## Stutter Like

Around the steeple beyond the stone stairs

refrain spilling forth      rakishly this

this and all a self thinks     and tastes

crouched on some pond

In suturing gather back

downing felt things

The pedal part of the organ

pressed down     to hear means the moon is a horn

or the threshold I rest in

this repeat     gorgeous when genuflecting I am

a cross atop a butte     stutters into night

again     genuflectingly gorgeous   I am

gorgeously genuflecting

**Kate Schapira**

## Between the wheel and the amount

*in response to Jay Snodgrass's "Steam Engines"*

Lubricated with blood
(the move to attribute hawks,
hits, evaporates. You might get two
urges that seem in
opposition: rip and seam of new
tissue as cruelty
bulks in the muscle
proto-plan hidden in the plan
you didn't tell, expedient.
Crows on the railing
anticipate all-day
trashy delights. The spread admits
guilt wedges
open the seat and optics of judgment:
conflation of persons and aid, twin
blades parting each other,
accusation and precision.)
Official candors gone to blood

# Kate Schapira

## On Response

When I started to write this, I worried because responding seemed like showcasing me rather than the poem—as soon as the poem's over, I switch to what I feel about it, or how it affects me, rather than what it's saying, doing, or being. But what I think once changes the landscape of what I think the rest of the time. Reading a poem is like adding a plant or digging a hole. Response is a tracking device for the changes that a poem made in my topography. It's full disclosure. It can answer the questions the poem raises, or be a question to its answers; it can be a footnote or an amendment; it can pick at a hangnail the poem starts. And it makes me answer for my reading, answer to the poem, risk exposure of the map.

Jay's poem, like its title, felt inexorable to me—a machine pounding in the direction of its conclusion. This produced a perverse desire in me to pry it open and add to the works, with the possible consequence of altering the poem's motion or direction. I chose to wedge my poem between two lines that ended with the same eyeball-jerker word, "blood", and that seemed to provide a hinge for his. My poem contains this idea of opening and exposing the works, whether metal or organic, and what happens when what's usually internal is exposed to air, light, and severance. I think it also asks who's driving, what's the motive power, why is the conclusion foregone?

Vines on the side of a house, phone conversations about taking the rap for somebody else: we also respond to things that aren't poems. So response treats the poem as a real thing or life, one more thing in the world.

**Paul Siegell**

## Patchwork Acrobatics: Harlequin Period Typos

*loosely constructed with concepts introduced by Bruce Covey*
*and his "Reveal" series*


Picas soak as art exhibition marks diplomatic anniversary
Picas soap often in individuals with psychological disturbances
Picas sober now those painstaking programs no longer exist
Picas socialize not normally regarded as nutritive, like dirt

Picas society reads, "US bridge collapse blamed on pigeons"
Picas soda has a well-known problem that is incompatible to
Picas sodium sips vinegar by the cup as beverage with meals
Picas sofas offer late-deal holidays to worldwide destinations

Picas SoHo creates a natural working environment so one can make
Picas sojourn his real name's sumthin else altogether but not entirely
Picas solar scrambles magpie eggs in the anagram of "sailor cap"
Picas sold is thinking of returning items regardless of store policy

Picas soldier on the Americas gold mining linked to state terror
Picas sole is the original ballet flats designer beware of imitations
Picas solecism notes the crescent at one's nail base is called *lunula*
Picas solidify what design execution works best within this context

Picas soloist spares a painted thot for such pioneering *pierroting*
Picas solstice reaches out to eclectic audiences all across bohemia
Picas solution found that the recipe lies in building relationships
Picas soma avoids obscure acronyms in all its titles—save one

Picas sonar reveals only a portion of what the alter-ego performs
Picas sonata to respond to the resultant request of name resolution
Picas soprano contains an untitled hidden track after "Psoas Circus"
Picasso soul harlequin units of hidden human festival measurement

**Paul Siegell**

## "Pooch surprised me with tickets to the Barnes Foundation"

Pooch surprised me with tickets to the Barnes Foundation, "home to one of the world's largest collections of Impressionist, Post-Impressionist and early Modern paintings, with extensive holdings by Picasso, Matisse, Cézanne, Renoir and Modigliani, as well as important examples of African sculpture."

Colors up to stretching, opening the optic nerves. She knows how much museums get me every time. She's good like that. And then we came upon the Rose: Picasso social outcasts, acrobats, harlequins, marginalized circus artists. I was all about it. Reminded me of concert parking lots. Joy and jesters. And the repeating diamond pattern of the harlequins' outfits got me thinking of a neat way to format a poem.

And, so did the "Reveal" sequence that Bruce Covey was cooking up all over the Internet. Turning set after set of everyday themes (i.e., Horse Less Review #4, "Reveal 54: Nutrition") into poems cut from Google's toys? Heck yeah! All those random, hilarious juxtapositions built on "I'm Feeling Lucky" lists. Each line has a common backbone, but each line seems to exists completely unto itself. Makes for some great sounding work, plus it's fun to try to come up with connections. And I thot... well, I could do that. With my own little twist on it, of course.

Justin Taylor & Bill Hayward

AMBROS ADELWARTH

*of is but of*

barely any recollection

well known to believe

the great upheaval

confirmed and

enhanced the general murmur

entirely free of meanings

vanished for good


I knew nothing throughout the summer

months incurably weeping with us

in the middle one really did not know

a complete disaster streaming


trees sped past us in the light

without looking through the dark
opening (how are you? I am fine!)
without fail a death
notice in the local paper

I imagined, as I grew up, that I too would
one day
live the different kind of everyday life

feet up on the table, children in the garden
               no one knew
The longer I studied
the photographs, the more urgently
I sensed a growing need to learn
the lives of the people in them

territory covered

indistinguishable          old women visit

summer

    always giving everything

    just enough, all told

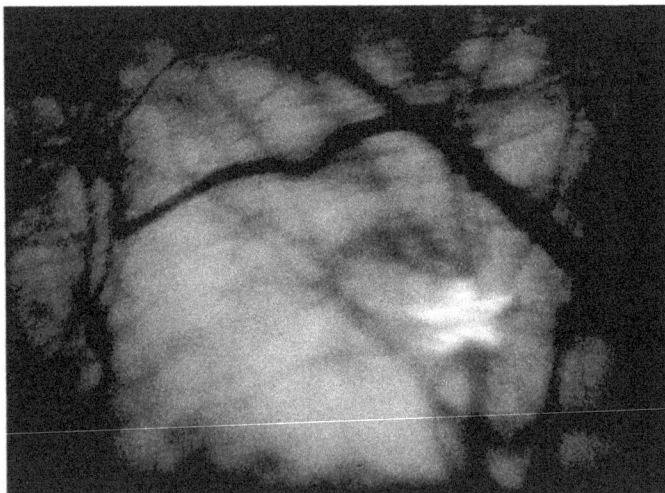

a child with a cross over her head

anxiety, departure          always one thing

after another

    as if a quite new and altogether more

    significant story were now beginning

the youngest rosehips cut open

the hairy seeds

    in a washtub

put the red flesh of the hips through
the press
the beauties enthusiastically praised
in the moonlight scarcely certain:

     initiated into all
the secrets of the special             All I know
of her is that she had a career in misfortune

         floating house

Something about archery       a good deal
the call to the subject      no wonder everything
seemed unfamiliar
and incomprehensible
a sense of unstoppable        February
       storms

the sunshot morning mists
       paper flowers full of hope

And the very next
day I was on the top of the tower

                      curvatures and slopes

                      so low and inky

                      more slowly

                      telling tales


I'm afraid I don't know much

        notorious

        eternal

        destroyed

        anyone could see

        the edge of the truth

submerged as if nothing is almost over

I thought: if you

just stayed                 now and then


seconds from out of mists     Of course

I do not know what was really going on


the flesh of the years unparalleled

in a whirl growing ever headier

eyes half closed

I cannot tell                you anything


an attempt to regain appears to have failed in every

respect a labyrinth with all its mirror reversals

a sort of collective oasis
amongst the spectators
craning round the terrible thing

In mid October the snows began
vast pine forests
impenetrable heights his clenched
bite when darkness fell where he faded

These things happened

the pendulous syllable holding court

unfathomable
like the room in this photograph

you may know an illness
which causes memories to be replaced
by a great need

he could no longer
coax the mirror I carried thinner
and thinner, lopsided black
exhaust growing smaller
and smaller
that mirror
still making
my notes on the inconsolable          the idea remained

to waste my air

I was wary
        I finally went
I ought not
        I felt
I and I
      the place names from the ruins of another world
overtaking, repeatedly
      a place in their hearts as a plateau rising to
some height

a patchwork flooded in the trembling dark,
distant longing for thoughts across
      an eternity untouched by certain place names

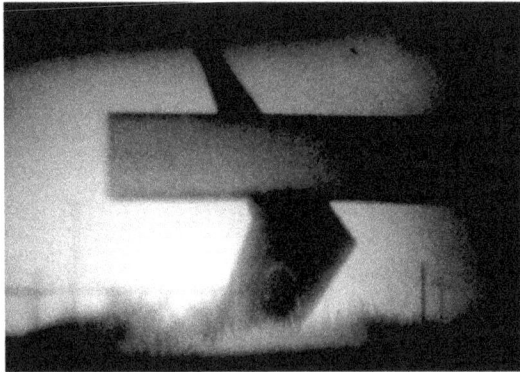

panoramic, streaked

heaving shadows filled with rushing sound
not, as I supposed at first,
the wretchedness extravagant

a diagnosed tendency to the fact of absence

these broad improvements
the madhouse multiplying
without cease beyond the trees

nowadays I place
all my hope in caving in
I have a dream of collapse
I see everything simultaneously
hollowed out under the surface blind
armies of the very last come down
spectacle in safe detention I believe
annihilation merely proof of corruptibility

        a picture of unoccupied houses
strange open interiors
            condemned to waiting for their dust


American century              a sea view
at once outsize and miniature           kaleidoscopic
afternoons and evenings       sacrificed       trying to
out-manoeuvre Fortune                    the most exotic
couples or groups beyond the light      me through the
haze, staring    and everyone was whatever
gentlemen ceded and lay where they could
I fatigued       I thought       or else really
the latest papers were silent somewhat
downcast and dejected as
if altered a point of stillness in the ceaseless

artistes of both sexes                              tycoons

magnates          planters          a wave

Things were happening

                              I heard people

the crowd one vast sea swelling cresting like crowns

that ebb darkly  the loveliest apart from all the rest

gleaming in the muted atmosphere

the pros and cons of all these theories

astounding eloquence contrasted with total lack

transparent besieged sex of morning beach merged

into sea, sea into sky an arduous task I should

probably never have accomplished a veil in the lagoon

very restless

beautiful

good

Later, low

a fire repairing

to the ruins of the fortifications

beneath the canopy out of time

and at the same time

the thin sickle above us where the Gods pass

I can write if I look straight up
I can scarcely believe
in the distinct orchestral music
behind the shadows of stairs and rooms

a paradise of slopes and groves

you climb forever and find yourself

enter a house
amidst the life and the silence
claims whole districts of the city
we unexpectedly have a distant view of
heartbeat
I imagine myself home again . . . the circular pause
as if the wheel had not yet been invented or are we
        no longer a part of time?

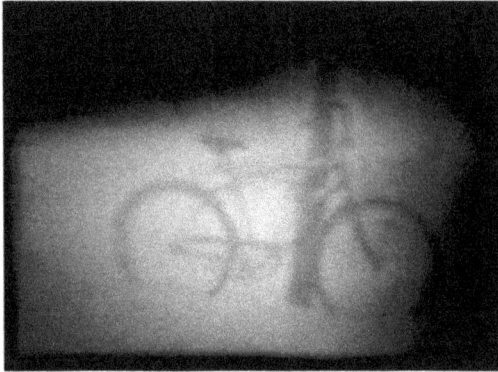

hall    walls    rooms  a ghost house              steps
a rooftop        an ancient vine        so close
we have never heard
the whispering of a far-off multitude
the demands of idleness        time and again
a soul entered by the half-light
        within the half-dark
both leading us to an alley              here and there
farther apart and altogether
the whole of the Holy Land              rocks
trees    a shrub        a meagre clump of weeds
great rolling emptiness        the promised city
in the distance          rocks            the desert
our horses      his duties      the rooms

one cannot say what period or part
of the world one is in numerous dreams
with strange voices and shouts

the city all in all a devotional

carvings and junk the faithful hordes pulverized
tallow-and-soap        bone-and-hide
coagulated heaps        blackish-brown dried scorched
establishments

in the centre of the city are the printing works

aisles transepts chapels shrines altars

crooked legs        a morass

from the miasma       a withered vineyard     a wild

olive tree, a thorn bush

               washed in such a flood of light!

the guidebook of the world       dry stone

and remote idea      the people have all they want

glorious gardens      bright palm groves

watercourses and pastures    vine leaves over

the pathways

belsséd are blank pages      the account of

the dream one wrongly imagines

fire and brimstone salt and ashes molten

lead that moonlit aura of the

blesséd bird of evening
like mere traces of overthrown cities

a little thicket
in an utterly beautiful curve

Memory a kind
of dumbness

towers whose tops are lost

Justin Taylor

## Note on Process

This poem is an excerpt from a larger manuscript, an erasure of W.G. Sebald's *The Emigrants*. Typical erasure manipulates an already-existing text by eliminating most of it, until a relatively small selection of words stands out on the largely redacted page. Rather than use a marker to erase the material I didn't want, I chose to use a highlighter to illuminate what interested me most. I transcribed all the highlighted material into a Word document, then set to work paring it down, further and further, relying on the delete key to bring disparate bits of text into closer contact than they were ever meant to have.

The poems' visual dimension hopes to evoke the look and feel of a traditional erasure, but the arrangement of words on the page is entirely artificial—a kind of highly constrained use of the cut-up method. Each poem in the manuscript corresponds to a chapter in the Sebald book, and the text of each poem is derived entirely from material in that chapter. In fact, my use of cut-up was limited entirely to deletion. The sequence of the prose has been entirely preserved. For example, the individual words in a phrase such as "the pendulous syllable holding court" may appear pages apart in *The Emigrants*, but if you were to read the book you would encounter the word "pendulous" sometime prior to encountering the word "syllable," and this is true of every word in *Notes*.

Eventually, I realized there was still something missing from my manuscript. Readers of Sebald know that his books all have a prominent visual component to them. Dozens of images—photographs, newspaper clippings, postcards, diary entries, landscapes, etc.—interrupt, augment, complicate, and otherwise supplement his texts. Rarely do Sebald's images serve a purely—or even primarily—illustrative function. Their relationship to the text tends to be both tenuous and ambiguous; sometimes the text will address a given image, but frequently no mention is made. Certainly, there are no captions.

I began to feel that my poems lacked a visual element comparable to that in the original source material. I decided to show the manuscript to my friend, Bill Hayward, a photographer and filmmaker whose work I admire very much. Happily, Bill liked Notes, and agreed to illustrate the poems with his photographs. This notion of "illustration" soon blossomed into something much more interesting: a fully collaborative image-text with two authors. This new phase of the project is at this writing—ongoing. Bill and I have worked together to select images that resonate with the poems and with each other. Our aim is to re-create, or at least refer directly to, the visual dimension of Sebald's work. But only at the level of form. At the level of content, we look for images which will double down on the operation my erasure attempts to perform on Sebald's novel: a push away from his themes and concerns of the source material, toward something neither suggested by nor wholly reconcilable with that from which it came. But still, in the end, undeniably its child.

**William Walsh**

# The Tepper Question: Isn't He Going Out?

A derived text sourced from *Tepper Isn't Going Out* by Calvin Trillin, 2001

Going out? Are you going out? Was it something that might simply come to him, after all these years? Now that he wasn't trying it several evenings a week under the pressure of Hector's watchful eye, might it just appear, the way a smooth golf swing sometimes comes inexplicably to duffers once the tension of their expensive lessons has ended? He's not going out? What do you mean he's not going out? Something in black, sir? How about this lovely number in black? Wouldn't it all look alike? How many hours must they spend every week sorting it out? Hey, are you going out or not, man? Or is that where you live? Is that car, like, rent controlled? Are you looking for a spot? What have you done with our grandson? Did he run away from home? Have you put him in foster care? Is that what you're doing, Daddy, running away from home? You go from the office to the garage that you pay for by the month, you get your car out, and you park it where you have no particular reason to be? Guess what? Daddy, I don't want to be pushy or anything, but what if I asked a fairly direct question: What, exactly, are you doing here? You mean like some old duffer who keeps thinking of his high-school football triumphs and ends up drunk late at night on the football field of his youth? Do you know what Aunt Harriet told Mom? Daddy, you're not having some sort of mid-life crisis, are you? Daddy, what should I tell Mom? You want to let me in, Eddie, so I can serve the people of this great city to the best of my ability? Didn't we have a security check yesterday? The mayor particularly worried about forces of disorder this week? Grandmother's maiden name? Do you have a reason to believe I'm not me? How do you know what the iris of my right eye is supposed to look like? Remember that second shot that seemed like a real close-up? You mean the mayor was this worried about the forces of disorder three years ago? Just look into the machine, willya, Mike? What are you muttering about there? What? Mayor? Was he getting repeaters? Isn't that proof? What kind of person would just happen to have four quarters in his pocket? How you doin'? How are you? Are you waiting for somebody? Just here, parking? You're just here parking because you feel like, and if someone wants the spot, it's too bad, because it's your spot, and it's a legal spot—right? Can you imagine? Oh? Do you mind if I sit with you for a minute? Why not? Talent? But have you ever seen Herman slice lox? The one who used to wear the badge saying, HERMAN THE ARTISTIC SLICER? Do you know what I really want to be? It didn't sell? It didn't sell? Can I interrupt you for a minute, Murray? How long you been here now, Arnie? An apple corer? What's the item he's selling? You put it around your neck and supposedly you sleep better because your head doesn't loll over and when you wake up you don't have a stiff neck? Is that the one? The thing is around your neck and the airport maps are on the thing and you're supposed to read the thing? So what's the problem? I don't suppose Barney's maps are detailed enough to show where you go to look for your lost baggage? May I ask you how old you are? You tried luggage—

right? Compasses? Am I interrupting? What's he selling now? What else does it do? Why don't you give a mainframe-computer-repair trade magazine list a shot? How's it going, Murray? How about you? Magic? So you and Ruth had a talk? I mean is there anything that's troubling you here? My God, how much could we have saved by not having to redo one word on the door? So what was the other function of the thing Barney's selling? Guess when I next have to move the car? What secret fraternity honk, by the way? I don't suppose you're going soon, are you, Murray? And draw attention to myself? Anything special bothering you, Murray? You and Ruth okay? Ruth? So what happens? Everything okay at the office? Are those turkeys still hiring you to sell their tchotchkes? They haven't caught on yet? Is it the Dodgers, Murray? Are you out here because you're still mad that they moved the Dodgers to L.A.? You want to know why it doesn't make any sense? So are you lost or what? But you don't find me still mad about it, right? Whatever happened to having a chat on a park bench? Whatever happened to having a chat on the stoop? What? You mean I should write letters, the way you wrote the owners of the Dodgers when they were talking about going to Los Angeles? Does this mean I should go sit in my car in Times Square? Is that going to be your report to Ruth? You don't see the harm? So you want to have a beer? Moishe in the Middle? What are you, Shanahan—some kind of rube? That's all? Why would you bet with the card down again? You don't think dropping the glove business means that he might be thinking of running for governor or senator instead of mayor, do you? You mean as opposed to a substantial issue like whether people should hail taxis from the sidewalk instead of the street?

But will the Wacko run against him? Remember the great exchange with the cardinal at the Catholic Charities dinner? What was the exchange with the cardinal? You mean it can spot a guy with a bug up his ass? What else would someone like you have to do? Are you going out or not? You're not going out? Whadaya—live there? You one of these homeless bastards, except you've got a car? I guess you're not going out—huh? Would it be okay if he sat with you for a few minutes? Why not? A scheme for marketing StediSoke to Generation X? Sort of? You mean you report part of the story and let the readers imagine the rest, or do you mean you don't have a job? Why is it that reporters covering an election campaign write almost exclusively about who might win, even though we're all going to know that the night of the election anyway? Not about politics? The paper calls itself a rag? Postmodern? Why not? Can I interrupt you for a moment, Murray? What about lettuce dryers? You're thinking that Barney Mittgin can sell his map-pillows with a list of people who have sent away for lettuce dryers? What? What was it last time we talked— gardening gloves? Magazine? There's enough to write about lettuce drying to have a magazine? Did you ever hear of a newspaper called the East Village *Rag*? What kind of a name is that for a newspaper anyway? Is Murray Tepper one of those people who is mad as hell and isn't taking it anymore? Is he trying to escape from a messy situation at home? Connective tissue of our society? When did Barney Mittgin start talking like that? Howard? Is there something I've missed about you all these years? Mee-dyum wher-ah? So, you found any decent spots lately or are you still spending a lot of time circling around the block? Could that be? Do you remember when we ran into those two Vassar girls wandering around Washington Square, and we didn't think they'd be very impress if we said we were just two schlemiels going to NYU on the ass end of the G.I. Bill so we told them we went to West Point? Remember that? Hey, what's this I hear about your friend Murray Tepper parking his car for pleasure? So what now? No, I mean what do I tell them? When people ask me about it, and I can't claim that you're an imposter, what do I tell them? Do you know what your son-in-law now thinks this is all about? What am I angry about? Am I angry that my daughter married someone who talks like that? I know you think your son-in-law has some mushy ideas, but all this isn't that you're angry about something, is it? So what do you think? About Sixty-eighth Street? What? You're putting me on, right? But who really knows? That's a joke, right? Mr. Tepper? Murray Tepper? Are you Mr. Tepper who goes and parks sometimes? How do you know me? Why not? Do you mind if I ask you a question? Are you also interested in mathematics? How about chess? Do you play chess? I don't suppose you're interested in exotic sorts of foods, too? What sort of extreme steps? Another musician? Do you find that other musicians of your acquaintance are also good at electrical things? Why, exactly, are you telling me this? But why particularly me? Why are you parked here today? And do you intend to leave? What do you mean, sit down there? What's the latest we've got on a head-to-head? Murray, could you pass the salt? Murray, do you want this shirt to go to the laundry or what? What do you think about going back to England sometime this summer? You don't have anything that would keep you here, do you? Keep me here? Like what? Maybe some project at the office, or maybe Howard wants to take off in September, or some activity or something? Some activity? Then

she said, Murray—it was the serious Murray—if we go to England, would you still

want to …you know…read the paper in the car? You mean go out parking in the

evenings? You mean you do it here because of something about the parking

situation? You know what I thought at first, Murray—when you first started going?

What? Then I thought: Murray? Did he try to park? What kind of rules did you

have? Parking rules? Yeah, you know: alternate-side parking? Meters? Is it

important? You know why? You were born here? And I told him the point of this

call was that my uncle didn't have a pension, so how could he have a pension

number? If so, was there some way to find the man, whose name Tepper didn't

know? How would he know? Why must they pester us with those cards? Whadaya,

holding office hours in there or something? You looking for a fat lip, or what? Can I

get up now? Is that a buzz I'm hearing? Would you say that sound is a soft buzz or

just sort of a loud tingle? How would you describe that sound? What sound? You're

not, for some reason, holding a tiny dagger in your mouth, are you, Mike? You think

I've swallowed a miniature Sikh for some reason and he left his tiny dagger in my

mouth on the way down? You think I've got designs on trimming the mayor's

toenails or something? Your retainer? What are you doing with a retainer? Teresa,

Shanahan said, does it occur to you that we may be approaching the area that some

might consider invasion of privacy? Teresa, can I go now? They can't run a check of

violations in a week? You think we haven't heard that one before? You think you're

dealing with a bunch of farmers here, Luis? It's legal now to carry on a business in your car? No license is required? Are you telling me that a shoemaker could just put some tools in the backseat and set up shop? What about the honest tradesmen who have to pay rent on their premises and city sales tax on their transactions? What about them? You may remember the knife sharpeners who used to go around in little trucks, conducting their business in the street? Any ideas? Am I to assume that nobody has any ideas about how to stop this? What do you have on this, Mike? And? So how come, then, it didn't buzz the other day? What didn't buzz? Why? Would that really be convenient? Editorial in the *Post*? Are you going to tell me about the complications of some places No Parking Eight A.M. to Eleven A.M. and other places saying No Parking Eleven A.M. to Two P.M.? Remember me from the restaurant today? I wonder, if you have a few minutes, you'd mind if I joined you? Apparently? You know what I mean? So you can't really comment very well on your wife's stories? Do you mean I should look for something in my wife's work that I can truly get excited about? *Who's crazy now?* So, was Yesboss really smashed up against the car when you got there? But what can Ducavelli get out of this? Going against Tepper is bound to be bad for his numbers—right, Mike? I mean, is there any way this could be good for his numbers? So why is Ducavelli doing this? Why does a compulsive person spend a lot of time organizing his bolts and screws and nuts and nails by size when he knows perfectly well there are better ways to spend his time? Do you realize what you're saying? Am I interrupting, Murray? And? I can't remember—is he an accountant? Well, Tepper finally said, what can I do for you, Howard? Is the summons something to worry about? Are there still a lot of letters coming in? Murray, Gordon said, where's this all going—this parking? I mean,

what's going to happen? This is Sy Lambert, the big agent, if I may ask? Murray, I

hope you don't mind my asking—you're not planning to drive there, are you? I'm

supposed to go up to the West Side, get my car, and drive it down to Fifty-seventh

Street, to a block that's going to be No Parking Nine to Seven at best? You got any

identification? You know why? Do you know the mayor? Who said anything about

writing? Ralph? Shall we turn that off? What are we to make of all this? Ralph?

What lesson? What harm is he doing? The kids are coming for lunch, right? Are you

going out to park? Murray, is it okay—I mean with the police and all? Are you going

down to Houston Street in front of Russ & Daughters? While you're down there,

why don't you pick up a pound of herring salad and a whitefish? A nice whitefish?

What kind of business is this? Miss Goldhurst? Remember Mr. Hogan, the gym

coach? You come in here from Queens to get lox? How many of my old fifth-graders

make the newspapers? What's your game here, Murray? Game? Are we putting

law-abiding citizens who have broken no law whatsoever behind bars now for what

we believe might be their intentions? What makes you think my client is here to

contravene the order against unlicensed demonstrations or exhibitions? You were?

May I serve you, Mr. Tepper? Any particular whitefish? Richard, do you want some

whitefish? Max, you want some whitefish? What new tooth? How did things go

down there this morning? There were television trucks? Were they there because of

you? What do you think, Max? We want you to do whatever makes you happy, but

can I just ask if you see this as something you'll always do? Always? Wanna see my new tooth? Mr. Tepper? Is she G.F.T. level? So what did you tell him? Why else would he have given up that spot? So what is it you wanted to see me about? Can I ask you a question about that? Do you go to some of the functions the mayor has in Gracie Mansion? So how do you find a spot when you go to one of these functions? What favor did you have in mind? I don't suppose you have a nephew who you think might be good in some city job? Or maybe you've got a building permit application that needs a little expediting? If you're trying to sell something that appeals specifically to rich people—let's say one of these rare-wine-of-the-month clubs—do you just send a mailing to everyone in the 10021 ZIP code anyway and not worry about hitting a lot of not-so-rich people who happen to live there because they have rent-controlled apartments? Best fund-raising list for the Republican National Committee? Exactly where on Seventy-eighth Street, Mr. Tepper? Tell me, is it difficult to park around there these days? Still a lot of Diplomatic Plates Only in that area? Murray, you're not very comfortable with this Lambert, are you? Even if there's a series of books? For your sake? Touch? Are you declaring for Congress? Declaring for Congress? I am? Miss Goldhurst really said that about my mark in deportment? You glued them to the floor? Mee-dyum wher-ah? And, by the way, can you get gefilte fish on the regular sushi special, or would that be an extra charge? There's enough advice for a book? Did I already tell you about the cottage? What are we saying? Mr. Tepper, he asked at one point, did you ever—if you were in the middle of an interesting story in the paper or perhaps an interesting conversation with somebody who dropped in to talk to you while you were parking—notice that the meter had run out and therefore go out and put more money in the meter? You mean that, for example, it's a one-hour meter and I've already put enough money in for one hour but the hour is up, do I go put in more money to get maybe another hour? Are we having a meeting? Howard? Do my eyes deceive me, or are you smiling? My list? What do you mean my list? Remember? What's the connection? What's the connection between accountants and designer jeans? What's the connection between the nose-hair clipper and the newsletter? Who knows? We've had calls? In play? His principals? And what did you say about your principals? What's the matter? Do you think it's all right to rent out their names? We live in a... what do you call it? Should I just sit down in this thing? How do you know that I haven't secreted in one of my body orifices a tiny penknife with which I intend to carve out the mayor's gizzard? But Trotskyite? What do the numbers look like? And you think this is from Tepper? So how do you suggest that I handle this Tepper problem? Then the sale of Worldwide Lists doesn't entail you and your partner staying on to run it for a period of time? And no series of advice manuals? No speaking tours? And, if I might ask, where will your car be while you're in England? What shall I say? You did used to park some times on Cooper Square, right? What would you think of that theory? Didn't you always used to take the overnight flight? If we're both keeping an eye out, what does it hurt? Do you want to stop at the newsstand and pick up the *Post* for the plane? The *Post*?

## BIOGRAPHIES

**Erik Anderson**'s creative and critical work has appeared in *American Letters & Commentary, Sleeping Fish, The Laurel Review, Trickhouse, The Recluse, Jacket, Rain Taxi, Witness, The Collagist, The Poetry Project Newsletter, Parcel* and many others. His book, *The Poetics of Trespass*, is forthcoming from Otis Books/Seismicity Editions in 2010.

**Cynthia Arrieu-King** is assistant professor of creative writing at Stockton College. Her poems are forthcoming in *Black Warrior Review, LIT*, and *The Lumberyard*. She lives near the Pine Barrens, but hasn't yet run into the Jersey Devil.

**Sarah Bartlett** lives in Portland, OR. Her chapbook (co-written with Chris Tonelli), *A Mule-Shaped Cloud*, was published by horse less press in 2008. Her recent work has appeared or is forthcoming in *Coconut, Sir!, Sixth Finch, Diagram*, and elsewhere. Poems co-written with Emily Kendal Frey have appeared in *sub-Lit, Portland Review, Caffeine Destiny, Alice Blue*, and *Bat City*.

**Eric Baus** is the author of *The To Sound* (Verse Press/Wave Books) and *Tuned Droves* (Octopus Books). He lives in Denver and edits Minus House chapbooks.

"WARSAW" and "FLORES" are from **THE BOWLING**, a collection of bowling by **Sommer Browning** and **Brandon Shimoda**, of the east and west coasts, connected by love and confusion for fine wooden lanes, entrancing lights, varnish, polish, skill cranes and poetry. As THE BOWLING, Sommer and Brandon will also be appearing in *The Corduroy Mtn.* and *past simple*. When not as THE BOWLING, Sommer and Brandon curate events, edit, write and draw, on the wood of split happening the coasts' endless motions.

**Peter Boyle** (b. 1951) lives in Sydney. His first collection of poetry *Coming home from the world* (1994) received the National Book Council Award and the New South Wales Premier's Award. Other collections include *The Blue Cloud of Crying* (1997) and *Museum of Space* (2004). His most recent book *Apocrypha* (2009) is an extensive collection of poems and other texts by a range of imaginary authors. Boyle is also a translator of French and Spanish poetry.

**Adam Clay** is the author of *The Wash* (Parlor Press, 2006) and *A Hotel Lobby at the Edge of the World*, forthcoming from Milkweed Editions. He co-edits *Typo Magazine*.

**Thomas Cook** is in Albany, NY, edits *Tammy*, and enjoys the White Burgundy of 2004.

**Bruce Covey**'s fourth book of poetry, *Glass Is Really a Liquid*, will be published by No Tell Books in 2009. He lives in Atlanta, Georgia, where he teaches at Emory University, edits Coconut Poetry, and curates the What's New in Poetry reading series.

**MTC Cronin** has written numerous collections of poetry (including several co-written with fellow-Australian poet, Peter Boyle) and a number of volumes of avant-garde cross-genre micro-essays. She currently lives, with her partner and three young daughters, on an organic farm (specializing in fresh Spanish produce) in the hinterland of Queensland's Sunshine Coast, Australia.

**Mark DeCarteret**'s work has appeared in the anthologies *American Poetry: The Next Generation* (Carnegie Mellon Press), *Brevity & Echo: Short Short Stories by Emerson College Alums* (Rose Metal Press), *Thus Spake the Corpse: An Exquisite Corpse Reader* (Black Sparrow Press) and *Under the Legislature of Stars—62 New Hampshire Poets* (Oyster River Press) which he also co-edited. This past April he was selected as the seventh Poet Laureate of Portsmouth, New Hampshire.

**DZ Delgado** lives and works in San Francisco. His collaborative work appears in Sandy Florian's forthcoming *On Wonderland & Waste* published by Sidebrow.

**Jennifer K. Dick**, from Iowa, is the author of *Fluorescence* (Univ. of Georgia Press, 2004), the chapbook *Retina/Rétine* (Estepa Editions, Paris, 2005 with artwork by Kate Van Houten & trans by Rémi Bouthonnier), and the BlazeVox eBook *Enclosures* (2007: http://www.blazevox.org/ebk-jd.pdf). She also has work in 6 anthologies, including *12 x 12: Conversations in 21st Century Poetry and Poetics* (University of IA Press, 2009). Living in Paris, she has just completed her PhD at Paris III in Comp Lit, teaches for L'EHESS & Polytechnique, and co-curates the IVY Writers Paris reading series with Michelle Noteboom. She keeps a blog, http://jenniferkdick.blogspot.com/, & is part of the collaborative poetry blog http://rewords.blogspot.com. She also writes regular columns on poetics for *Tears in The Fence* in the UK.

**Camille T. Dungy** is author of *Suck on the Marrow* (Red Hen Press, 2010) and *What to Eat, What to Drink, What to Leave for Poison* (Red Hen Press, 2006). She is co-editor of *From the Fishouse: An Anthology of Poems that Sing, Rhyme, Resound, Syncopate, Alliterate, and Just Plain Sound Great* (Persea, 2009) and editor of *Black Nature: Four Centuries of African American Nature Poetry* (UGA, 2009). Dungy is associate professor of Creative Writing at San Francisco State University.

**Sandy Florian** is the author of *Telescope* (Action Books), *32 Pedals & 47 Stops* (Tarpaulin Sky), *The Tree of No* (Action Books), *Prelude to Air From Water* (Elixir Press), and *On Wonderland & Waste* (Sidebrow Press). She lives in San Francisco where she is an affiliate artist at Headlands Center for the Arts and works as one of the "other" editors at *Tarpaulin Sky Journal*.
Please visit her blog at http://boxingthecompass.blogspot.com.

**Emily Kendal Frey** lives in Portland, Oregon. She is the author of AIRPORT (Blue Hour 2009).

**Annie Finch**'s books of poetry include *The Encyclopedia of Scotland, Eve, Among the Goddesses,* and *Calendars* (shortlisted for the Foreword Poetry Book of the Year Award). Her other works include the definitive translation of the *Complete Poems of Louise Labé,* the essay collection *The Body of Poetry: Essays on Women, Form, and the Poetic Self* (in the Poets on Poetry Series from University of Michigan Press), and five influential anthologies of poetics, most recently *Multiformalisms: Postmodern Poetics of Form* coedited with Susan Schultz. Her collaborations with theater, art, and dance include the libretto for the opera Marina. She is Director of the Stonecoast MFA Program in Creative Writing at the University of Southern Maine.

**Terita Heath-Wlaz** is currently an MFA candidate and writing instructor at the University of Florida. Her poems have recently appeared in *Cream City Review, Court Green, Ninth Letter, CutBank* and other journals.

**Erika Howsare** lives in Virginia, works as a newspaper editor and co-edits *the horse less review.* She holds an MFA from Brown University. A collaboration with Kate Schapira, *Roadblock/Sightlines,* is forthcoming as an online chapbook from The Cultural Society.

**Kirk Keen** is an organic poet, thus needs little watering. He's been lucky enough to have had poems published by good people like horse less press, sundress publications, and others. Kirk is from Portland, OR by way of Boston and west Texas.

**Kristi Maxwell** is the author of *Realm Sixty-four* (Ahsahta, 2008), *Elsewhere & Wise* (dancing girl, 2008), and *Hush Sessions* (Saturnalia, 2009).

**Gary L. McDowell**'s first collection of poems, *American Amen,* won the 2009 Orphic Prize and will appear in late 2010 from Dream Horse Press. He is also the author of two chapbooks, *They Speak of Fruit* (Cooper Dillon, 2009) and *The Blueprint* (Pudding House, 2005) and co-editor of *The Rose Metal Press Field Guide to Prose Poetry: Contemporary Poets in Discussion and Practice* (Rose Metal Press, 2010). His poems have appeared in various literary journals, including *Colorado Review, Indiana Review, The Laurel Review, New England Review, Ninth Letter, Poetry Daily,* and *Quarterly West.* He lives in Kalamazoo, MI with his wife and their young son, Auden.

**Seth Perlow** is a doctoral candidate in English at Cornell University. He studies twentieth-century poetry, new media, and critical theory. His poetry and translations have appeared in *elimae, Opium, textsound, Carousel,* and elsewhere. His chapbook, *Robot Portrait of Homo Futurus,* was published by P. S. Books in 2009. Current projects include owning a cat, reading books, and sleeping more.

**The Pines** have published correspondence, music, poems and stories in the United States and Australia. Their most recent release is *Black Sabbath Volume Four*, available in print and on vinyl. They are currently invested entirely in the fast-food franchise Arby's.

**Dani Rado** received her MFA in fiction writing from the University of Notre Dame in 2005. Her work has appeared in *Bloom*, *Harpur Palate*, and *SNReview*, among others. She currently attends the University of Denver.

**Andrea Rexilius** is currently working towards her PhD in Literature and Creative Writing at the University of Denver. Her poetry and essays have appeared or are forthcoming in *Bird Dog*, *Coconut*, *Colorado Review*, *How2*, *Minor American*, *P – Queue*, *Volt*, and elsewhere. She is the editor of the online journal *PARCEL* and Associate editor of the *Denver Quarterly*.

**Susan Scarlata**'s work has appeared in *Coconut*, *Conduit*, *Fence*, *Parcel*, *Sous Rature* and various other magazines. She recently completed her PhD at The University of Denver, and she holds an MFA from Brown University. Susan is the Editor of Lost Roads Publishers and lives in Wyoming where many of her neighbors are quadrupeds.

**Kate Schapira** is the author of *TOWN* (Factory School, Heretical Texts 2010) and several chapbooks with Flying Guillotine Press, Portable Press at Yo-Yo Labs, Cy Gist Press, Rope-A-Dope Press and horse less press, as well as her own kitchen-table imprint, In Hand Books. She runs the Publicly Complex Reading Series in Providence, RI.

**Ravi Shankar** edits *Drunken Boat*, online journal of the arts, co-directs the Creative Writing Program at Central Connecticut State University, has published a book of poems, *Instrumentality* (Cherry Grove, 2004), a collaborative chapbook, *Wanton Textiles* (No Tell Books, 2006), and has two chapbooks (*Voluptuous Bristle* & *Seamless Matter*) forthcoming in 2010. His second manuscript of poems, *Deepening Groove*, is the winner of the National Poetry Review Prize and will be out in Spring 2011. He co-edited *Language for a New Century: Contemporary Poetry from Asia, the Middle East & Beyond* (W.W. Norton & Co., 2008) and choreographs ballet russes with varied folk.

**Brandon Shimoda**'s collaborations, drawings and poems have appeared in print, online, on magnetic tape, vinyl and walls. He was born in 1978, in the San Fernando Valley, and lives now in the shadow of a chief hanged for murder.

**Paul Siegell** is the author of three books of poetry: *wild life rifle fire* (Otoliths Books, 2010), *jambandbootleg* (A-Head Publishing, 2009), and *Poemergency Room* (Otoliths Books, 2008). He is a staff editor at *Painted Bride Quarterly*, and has contributed to

*The American Poetry Review*, *Coconut*, *Rattle* and many other fine journals. He has also been featured in two national music and culture magazines, *Paste* and *Relix*, as well as elsewhere exciting. Kindly find more of Paul's work at ReVeLeR @ eYeLeVeL (http://paulsiegell.blogspot.com).

**Nate Slawson** designs books for Cinematheque Press. He is the author of the chapbooks *a mixtape called Zooey Deschanel* (linelinelineline, 2009) and *The Tiny Jukebox* (H_NGM_N Books, 2009). Recent work has appeared or is forthcoming in *diode*, *Typo*, *Forklift Ohio*, *Cannibal*, *DIAGRAM*, and other places.

**Mathias Svalina** & **Julia Cohen** are the collaborative authors of four chapbooks: *Sugar Means Yes* (forthcoming Greying Ghost Press), *When We Broke the Microscope* (Small Fires Press), *Force, Proximity, Repulsion* (forthcoming Cinematheque Press), & *You Are the Motor* (forthcoming Further Adventures).

**Justin Taylor** is the author of a collection of poems, *More Perfect Depictions of Noise*, and a book of short stories, *Everything Here is the Best Thing Ever*. http://www.justindtaylor.net/      **Bill Hayward** is a photographer and filmmaker who lives in New York City and Montana. His most recent book is a collection of "portraits of the collaborative self" entitled, *Bad Behavior* (Rizzoli). He is currently completing a new book of portraits entitled *The Human Bible*, and is also at work on a film entitled *Asphalt, Muscle & Bone*.

**Catherine Theis** is the author of the chapbook, *The Fraud of Good Sleep* (SUN SUN SUN Press). Her poems have appeared or are forthcoming in various journals, including *Action Yes*, *Columbia Poetry Review*, *Gulf Coast*, *LIT*, *Sonora Review*, and *Volt*. Catherine is the recipient of a 2009 Individual Artists Fellowship from the Illinois Arts Council.

**William Walsh** is the author of *Without Wax: A Documentary Novel* (Casperian Books, 2008) and *Questionstruck* (Keyhole Press, 2009). His stories and derived texts have appeared in *Lit*, *Caketrain*, *New York Tyrant*, *Quick Fiction*, *Annalemma*, *No Colony*, *Juked*, *Artifice*, and other journals. A short story collection titled *Ampersand, Mass.* is forthcoming from Keyhole Press in early 2011.

**Jess Wigent** and **Shawn Huelle** grill somewhere in the tangential point between peaches and infinity. They enjoy stoning zeroes and questioning bricks and glass (there mostly only to be questioned). They write all of their stories underneath your wallpaper or on the backs of beetles drunk on bottle labels.

www.ingramcontent.com/pod-product-compliance
Lightning Source LLC
LaVergne TN
LVHW011246080426
835509LV00005B/643